Pages 1 - 7: Scenes through the seasons:

◀◀◀◀◀ **Indian River Inlet**
◀◀◀◀ **Along The Brandywine River**
◀◀◀ **Gardens at Winterthur**
◀◀ **Bombay Hook Wildlife Refuge**
◀ **Brandywine Creek State Park**

To my mother and father,
Catherine and Fred Miller,
your example has shaped
the way I think and feel and believe.
To my wife, Enys, and son, Alex,
you are my inspiration in all that I do.

Images of DELAWARE

Special thanks to John M. Burris, Ben Pearce, and Frederick Miller.

Copyright 1998 Mike Biggs and Lise Monty
MILLER PUBLISHING, INC.

MILLER PUBLISHING, INC.
1201 N. Orange Street, Suite 200,
Wilmington, DE 19801
www.millerpublishinginc.com
info@millerpublishinginc.com

Published in 1998
Printed in Korea

Library of Congress Catalog Number 98-30751
ISBN: 0-9663337-0-5
First Edition October 1998

PHOTOGRAPHY: Mike Biggs
TEXT: Lise Monty
DESIGN DIRECTION: B. Ben Pearce
PUBLISHER: Frederick Miller

*I*mages of
DELAWARE

Photography by Mike Biggs/Text by Lise Monty

Foreword by
John M. Burris

Designed by Bernard Ben Pearce

PUBLISHED BY MILLER PUBLISHING, INC.
WILMINGTON, DELAWARE

This book was made possible through the generosity of the following :

Delaware State Chamber of Commerce

Bell Atlantic - Delaware, Inc.

The Chase Manhattan Bank

Artesian Resources Corporation

FMC Corporation

Greenwood Trust Company

Zeneca Inc.

M. Davis & Sons, Inc.

W. L. Gore & Associates, Inc.

Beebe Medical Center

Bancroft Construction Company

Standard Chlorine of Delaware, Inc.

Snyder, Crompton & Associates

Andersen Consulting LLP

Contents

Foreword

In 1867, William T. Burris, a Sussex County farmer, received a letter of commendation for his service to the Union Army during the Civil War. He was the earliest known Burris on record in the State of Delaware.

More than one hundred years later, seven generations of Burrises have made Delaware their home—as farmers, entrepreneurs, industrialists, politicians and community leaders—a journey that many other Delawareans have also taken. In many ways, the history of this particular family—my family—reflects the history of the state itself.

Like many other residents of the state, Edward Burris was a farmer like his father, William, growing tomatoes and corn in Lincoln downstate of the DuPont powerhouse in Wilmington. He had the equivalent of a sixth grade education, which nevertheless enabled him to thrive as a successful small farmer. As the Great Depression hit, his son John W. Burris decided it was crucial to expand the market for their produce; he bought a pickup truck, loaded it up with Burris farm goods, and drove up to Philadelphia to find a distributor. He found a willing partner in A&P grocery stores, cementing a relationship that would last over half a century. Now that Philadelphia was on board, John W. turned his vision toward Baltimore and points south. He soon created a system by which a ferryboat would take Burris Farm pickup trucks and produce to Baltimore across the Chesapeake Bay.

During that time, John W. also entered the political arena. He was first elected State Representative in the 1930s and then moved on to the Senate where he served from 1948-1952.

John E. ("Jack") Burris, John W. Burris's son and my father, caught the entrepreneurial spirit that took hold of most Delawareans. He started a poultry processing business and a frozen foods company to begin with, and then branched out into several other affiliated businesses, such as Burris Express (trucking) and Burris Refrigerated Services. From one employee with one basket of tomatoes six decades ago, the company has now grown to more than 500 employees.

As a former politician I served three terms as the State Representative for Milford beginning in 1976, first as Minority Leader, then Majority Leader. As a former businessman, working 17 years in the family business, I have been president of the Delaware State Chamber of Commerce since 1989. In these capacities, I have seen the state from every angle. I have encountered every problem, witnessed every setback, noted every issue—and rejoiced at every success. And there have been a number of successes.

In the 1970s, I was a member of the State Legislature when we passed the Financial Center Development Act, a monumental step forward for the state in terms of economic development. A series of initiatives designed to attract new business to the state as well as diversify its economic base, the FCDA succeeded beyond most people's wildest expectations. Double-digit unemployment dropped dramatically, population increased, and nearly everyone's business prospered.

Delaware was able to pull off this feat because it is a small state and its leaders have been able to think quickly and move even faster. Those who live in Delaware know that decision-makers can and will get things done because public-private partnerships are the norm, rather than the exception. People who live here—from the families who've made this their home for centuries to the recent college graduates who've been recruited from across the country—have tremendous ownership in the state, which pays big dividends in terms of our quality of life. When people come to Delaware, they never want to leave.

What does the state have to offer its citizens? For business-oriented folks, there is the business-friendly infrastructure put in place by our three previous governors: Delaware functions as one of the top small-business incubators in the country; it's an agribusiness powerhouse, home to thriving poultry and farm industries; it's a financial and legal services haven, with one of the busiest Chancery Courts in the country; it has first rate institutions of higher learning and a tremendous asset in Dover's Air Force Base. The state is so favorable for business that it was recently named the second best state for business, after Texas.

But business is not the only lure of the state: our flourishing tourism industry brings in nearly one billion dollars per year and shows no signs of abating. World-class museums, theater, art and music add up to more culture per capita than many states twice Delaware's size can offer.

Delaware's beach area, known as the "Nation's Summer Capital," continues to draw visitors and year-long residents in record-breaking numbers each year. And Delaware's protected nature reserves and greenways make this a special place for those who appreciate unspoiled beauty.

With all of these attractions, the State has managed to overcome the challenges of rapid growth by investing heavily in roads, schools, and other infrastructure. This ensures that Delaware will remain a place where future generations will continue to want to live.

My family has lived, worked and grown in the State of Delaware, a state that we believe is one of the most uniquely livable in the country. I welcome you to our state, to visit or to put down roots, and discover what makes this one of the best-kept secrets in America.

John M. Burris

The First Four Centuries

16th Century- Delaware's first people, the peace-loving Lenni Lenape Indians live here and throughout an area extending north to what is now New York City. Today, most of the surviving Lenni Lenape descendants live in Oklahoma, but some 1000 members of a related tribe, the Nanticoke, live in Sussex County, most in the area of Millsboro. Spaniards and Portuguese make early explorations of the Delaware coastline.

1609- Henry Hudson, an English explorer hired by the Dutch to find a shorter passage to Asia, enters and examines the Delaware Bay before sailing up the Atlantic Coast to the river that bears his name.

1610- The English ship captain Samuel Argall, coming from Jamestown, Virginia, is blown off course and sails into a strange bay which he names in honor of his governor, Lord de la Warr. It is doubtful that the Lord ever saw the bay, river, and state which today bear his name.

1630s- The Dutch come, the Swedes come, the Finns come, and later, the English. All praise the beauty of the land and the abundance of its natural resources and fight with one another over possession.

1631- Eleven years after the English pilgrims land at Plymouth, Massachusetts, the Dutch establish a fishing settlement named Zwaanendael, which means Valley of the Swans, near present-day Lewes. Zwaanendael Museum, built in 1931 to commemorate the town's 300th anniversary, celebrates the original settlement and 300-plus years of Lewes history.

1632- Captain David Pietersen de Vries comes from Holland to Zwaanendael to be the leader of the new colony. He finds it has been destroyed, the result of a misunderstanding between the Dutchmen and their Indian neighbors.

1633- De Vries writes glowingly about the area: "This is a very fine river and the land all beautifully level, full of groves of oak, hickory, ash, and chestnut trees, with many wild grape vines growing upon them. The river has a great plenty of fish— perch, roach, pike, and sturgeon—as in our Fatherland."

1638- The first Swedish immigrants to North America sail on the *Kalmar Nyckel* and the *Vogel Grip* up the Delaware River into a smaller river they name the Christina for their young queen. The colonists land at a place where rocks make a natural dock. Today those rocks are part of Fort Christina State Park in Wilmington, which perpetuates the memory of these first settlers and preserves "The Rocks" where they first landed. Adjacent to the park is an operational historical shipyard created to build a replica of the *Kalmar Nyckel*. Since it was launched in 1997, Delaware's Tall Ship has assumed a high profile not only in the First State but at various festivals in Baltimore, Philadelphia and Norfolk, Va., among other cities.

1638- The settlers in New Sweden, almost half of whom were Finns, introduce the construction of log houses to the New World.

1643- Johan Printz arrives in New Sweden as its new governor. A huge man weighing nearly 400 pounds, Governor Printz was a good leader who kept the little colony going for 11 years despite considerable adversity.

1655- Gov. Peter Stuyvesant of New Netherlands (comprising the present-day states of New York and New Jersey), considering New Sweden a commercial rival, decides to challenge the Swedes. The Dutch fleet takes over Fort Casimir (at the present site of New Castle) and then expels the settlers in New Sweden. The Dutch rule this area for only nine years, but during that time build a town they call New Amstel, which today is New Castle.

1664- The English seize the Dutch settlements. Under English rule, Delaware was at first governed as part of the proprietary colony of New York, and the town of New Castle was the local center of government.

1682- The Duke of York agrees to give William Penn what is now Pennsylvania and Delaware, called the Lower Counties. Penn had won claim to "all land located within a twelve-mile circle from the town of New Castle..." This defined the arc that still marks Delaware's northern boundary, the only such boundary in the country. Penn names Kent and Sussex counties for English counterparts. The court for Kent meets in what becomes the town of Dover on the St. Jones River; the court for Sussex County meets in Lewes, the new name for the old Dutch town of Hoerekil.

1698-99- Descendants of the first Swedish colony build Holy Trinity Church, affectionately known as "Old Swedes." Today it is recognized as one of the country's oldest church buildings still in regular use for worship. Established as a Swedish Lutheran Church, Old Swedes was placed under the jurisdiction of the Protestant Episcopal Church in 1791. Its mixture of historical and modern fixtures reflects the history of worship at Old Swedes, which began 300 years ago and continues today. The church yard predates the church by 60 years and was used as a burying ground for early settlers of Fort Christina. Among those buried there are three members of a distinguished Delaware family: James Bayard, Senator; Richard Bayard, first Mayor of Wilmington; and Thomas F. Bayard, Secretary of State under President Cleveland and later Ambassador to the

Court of St. James. Today, visitors may tour the church and the adjoining Hendrickson House, the historic home of a Swedish farmer, which was moved from near Chester, Pennsylvania, to the site in the 1950s.

1700- Parson Sydenham Thorne establishes the town of Milford, divided by the Mispillion River, which provides the transportation needed to grow its shipbuilding industry.

1704- The Lower Counties establish their own independent legislature which meets each year at the Court House in New Castle. The Court House was Delaware's colonial capitol and the meeting place of the State Assembly until 1777. The Declaration of Independence was read and the first Constitution of Delaware was drafted here in 1776. The Court House that stands today, one of America's most venerable buildings, was built in 1732 on the site of an earlier Court House. Built long before Philadelphia's Independence Hall or Boston's Faneuil Hall, it was Delaware's first state house and served as the New Castle County Court House from the days of the Penns until 1881. The Court House can be visited today and guided tours are available.

Early 1700s- In addition to the English, large numbers of Scotch-Irish come to Delaware, some as indentured servants. Welsh from the Isle of Wales settle on the Welsh Tract near Newark; immigrants from Germany come to Wilmington to work in the shipyards and factories; and Quakers move to Wilmington from Philadelphia. Africans also come to Delaware, the majority either as indentured servants or slaves working for their owners. Through the efforts of the Quakers, some of the slaves are set free.

1731- Thomas Willing founds a town on the banks of the Christina River which he calls Willingtown. He lays out the streets in a grid pattern, just as they were in Philadelphia. He puts the lots up for sale, but virtually no one comes. Finally, in 1735, William Shipley of Philadelphia buys land in Willingtown, recognizing its location as having good possibilities for trade. Many others follow, and by 1739, there are 600 people living here.

1739- The Penn family gives Willingtown a charter, allowing the town to hold markets and to organize its own government. The Penns change the town's name to Wilmington, in honor of the Earl of Wilmington, an important English official.

1742-1760s- Flour mills flourish on the banks of the Brandywine. Wheat purchased from area farmers is ground into flour, put in barrels and sent to market in the West Indies and Europe. The Brandywine mills are built and run by Quakers who live in Brandywine Village. Trade keeps expanding and so does the population. By the time of the Revolution, about 2000 people live in Wilmington.

1769- King George III approves the work of two English surveyors, Charles Mason and Jeremiah Dixon, establishing the Mason-Dixon line between Delaware and Maryland from north to south. This also settles a 70-year-old dispute between the Penn family and the Calverts of Maryland, who believed that the Lower Counties belonged to them.

1776—June 15- The Assembly of the Lower Counties, meeting in New Castle, votes for independence from England and from Pennsylvania. Since the American Bicentennial in 1976, the town of New Castle has marked "Separation Day " with public flag-waving and festivities that include a parade, concerts, regatta on the Delaware, and living history everywhere.

1776—July 1- Caesar Rodney, at home in Dover, receives a message that the Congress in Philadelphia will vote July 2 to accept a Declaration of Independence and that all Congressmen must vote. He immediately sets out on his horse and rides all night to get there in time to declare his vote for independence. A large statue in Wilmington's Rodney Square immortalizes the patriot's historic ride.

1777- Militia units from Delaware join in the fight for independence as the Revolutionary War continues. The only battle fought in Delaware was at Cooch's Bridge, along the road from Glasgow to Newark. Here General William Maxwell and his men, greatly outnumbered by the English who are advancing from Maryland to Pennsylvania, are forced to withdraw. During the Revolution, the British occupy Wilmington and seize the public treasury, and Delaware Bay is blockaded by the Royal Navy.

1787- Thirty delegates to the state's ratifying convention meet in Dover and officially accept the new U.S. Constitution, the first state to do so. Gathering at the Golden Fleece Tavern on Court House Square, now known as The Green, they disagree about many issues, but not on the need for ratification. Historians have called the unanimous opinion remarkable. And little did they know that more than 200 years later Delaware would still be capitalizing on its "First State" status.

1800- A young French chemist named Eleuthere Irenee du Pont arrives in the United States.

1802- E.I. du Pont acquires 95 acres of land along the Brandywine Creek from Jacob Broom to establish the E.I. du Pont de Nemours Company to manufacture black powder. It provided gunpowder for the military as well as for blasting and for hunting, becoming a leading producer of explosives.

1813- During the War of 1812, the English navy blockades the American coast. An English fleet blocks the channel from the Delaware Bay into the Atlantic Ocean. The English begin firing cannons at Lewes but do little damage since the majority of the cannonballs fall into a marsh. One chicken is killed and a cannonball hits one house but does not do serious damage. In fact, the "cannonball house" still stands in Lewes today. This was the last time Delaware was attacked by an enemy nation.

1829- The Chesapeake and Delaware Canal, connecting the Delaware River with the Chesapeake Bay, opens, expediting the shipping of goods between Baltimore and Philadelphia just as it does today. Many of the canals built at that time no longer exist, but the C&D, which has been enlarged several times, is busier than ever.

1829- The General Assembly passes the Free School Law, a move toward the development of tax-supported public education. Only white children can attend these schools.

1832- The first railroad in Delaware, the New Castle and Frenchtown Railroad, is completed. It crosses the Delmarva Peninsula just a few miles north of the Chesapeake and Delaware Canal.

1833- The state legislature charters the first college in Delaware—Newark College, which was for young white men exclusively. It became Delaware College and then the University of Delaware.

1838- The Philadelphia, Wilmington, and Baltimore Railroad, known as the P.W. & B., begins carrying passengers from Wilmington to the area's two largest cities, Philadelphia and Baltimore.

1850s- A third railroad begins transporting crops and people. The Delaware Railroad connects with the P.W. & B. and runs along the western part of the state through Middletown, Clayton and Harrington to Seaford.

1860- Though slavery is still legal in Delaware, it is becoming uncommon, and several citizens are involved in leading slaves to freedom. Despite pressure from the Confederacy to join its secession from the United States, the General Assembly votes to stay in the Union. Members say that since Delaware was the first to join the United States, it would be the last to leave it. The debate divides people in small towns and large, old friends and even families.

1861- War breaks out between the United States and the Confederate States. Soldiers traveling from Northern states go through Wilmington. At the train station, people cheer them and give them food. But south of Wilmington, pro-confederate people try to stop the soldiers from reaching Washington, D.C., by tearing up the railroad tracks.

1861-1865- About 12,000 men from Delaware join the Union Army; about 500 Delawareans join the Confederate Army. The Union soldiers from Delaware fight in some of the biggest battles of the war, including Gettysburg. Because Delaware is so close to the fighting, the Union builds a hospital in Wilmington, where many women volunteer to be nurses. Women also raise money to support the hospital. Fort Delaware on Pea Patch Island, which had been built to guard cities and towns from enemy ships, becomes a prisoner of war camp. Many of the prisoners die there. Today it is Fort Delaware State Park offering living history programs and a diversity of activities for visitors.

Post Civil War- Officially, slavery is ended, but equality for blacks is a long way off. It is virtually impossible for them to vote or get elected. A group of Wilmingtonians, both black and white, raise money to build schools for black people. But the state does not spend as much money on schools for black children as it does on schools for white children. Life for the average black changes little from the end of the Civil War to the next century.

1891- Delaware State College is founded in Dover as the first school in the state to give blacks a college education.

Turn of the century- The agricultural industry flourishes as farmers use the railroad to transport their blackberries, peaches, apples, potatoes, and tomatoes to big cities. Some of the produce goes to canneries, which become an important industry in southern Delaware.

Early 1900s- New inventions, including electricity and telephones, begin to change people's lives. The horse and buggy is gradually replaced by electric trolley cars, and for a privileged few, the automobile. But it's the railroad that northern Delawareans use to get to the beach. The new coastal communities of Rehoboth Beach, Dewey Beach, Bethany Beach and Fenwick Island are all newly founded.

1902- The Du Pont Company incorporates and moves away from the complete manufacturing of explosives to mass production and distribution of a variety of products, with new emphasis on research.

1906- The Du Pont Company, which has become the state's biggest business, erects the first large office building in Delaware in downtown Wilmington. It is headquarters for the large manufacturing company with factories all over the United States.

1911- T. Coleman du Pont receives authorization from the General Assembly to construct a modern highway from Milford to Wilmington at his own expense. Du Pont Highway, which is now Route 13, is completed in 1924.

1920s- Because trucks can travel rapidly on the new highway, farmers in Sussex County begin raising broiler chickens, which have become the dominant force in Delaware agriculture.

World War II- Some German U-boats, whose mission was to sink allied ships carrying supplies and troops to Europe, come close to the Delaware coast. To combat these enemy boats, the Army builds a series of watch towers along Delaware's seashore. Several still stand, including one observation tower in Cape Henlopen State Park which is open to the public. The New Castle County Army Air base, now the Greater Wilmington Airport, is used to ferry planes and supplies. Dover Airfield, now Dover Air Force base, is built to be used as a training field for pilots and for the secret testing of America's first rockets. Wilmington's shipyards make war supplies, including landing craft that brought soldiers and marines to enemy beaches. The country's three largest explosives makers, DuPont, Atlas and Hercules, supply most of the ammunition used by the United States Army and Navy. DuPont's nylon is used to make parachutes.

1947- General Motors opens its assembly plant in Elsmere and starts fulfilling the desire for a car or two in every driveway, fueled by the growth of suburban housing developments, shopping centers and industrial parks.

1951- Chrysler opens a plant in Newark to build military tanks. In 1956, it is converted to an automobile assembly plant.

1971- Following lengthy public debate, the Coastal Zone Act proposed by Governor Russ Peterson is adopted by the General Assembly. It outlaws all new heavy industry "incompatible with the protection of the natural environment" along the shoreline. Some have said that the Financial Center Development Act passed in 1981 is one payoff of the Coastal Zone Act because it forced the state to look for other businesses and industries, including banking.

1972- Delaware is the last state to abolish the whipping post. It had last been used in 1952.

1977-Pete du Pont moves from the U. S. Congress into the Governor's Office at a time when the state is reeling from successive blows to its economy and finances and its credit rating is the lowest in the country. He leads fiscal reform and economic development efforts that begin to turn things around.

1981- The Financial Center Development Act becomes law, giving credit-card banks the freedom to set interest rates and a big incentive to set up business in Delaware. More than 30 banks move their credit card operations to Delaware as a result of this legislation.

Dutch is spoken here, in spirit, at the
Zwaanendael Museum in Lewes, modeled
on the town hall of Hoorn in the Netherlands. It was built in 1931 to commemorate the 300th anniversary of the first
European settlement in Delaware. This site
was known as Zwaanendael or "valley of
the swans" to the Dutch who first established a fishing settlement here.

A cornerstone of Lewes's historical charm is Shipcarpenter Square, an enclave of private homes dating from 1720 to 1880 that were moved here from their original sites and restored. Across the street is the Lewes Historical Society's Historic Complex with several notable buildings including the Rabbit's Ferry House (right) and the Cannonball House, which was struck by a cannonball during the British bombardment of Lewes in 1813. Four Delaware governors are buried at St. Peter's Episcopal Church, which dates back to 1704. The present building, glorified by a beautiful sky, was consecrated in 1858 and restored to its original dignity in 1948.

In 1774 Odessa's leading citizen, tanner William Corbit, completed building his fine Georgian-style country house. His descendants maintained the house for more than 150 years until 1958 when a new owner, H. Rodney Sharp, restored it and donated it to Winterthur Museum, Garden & Library. Known today as the Corbit-Sharp House and open to visitors, it contains regional and family furnishings that reflect life from 1774 to 1818.

Odessa's Pump House recalls an earlier time when residents came here to the town's public water pump that is still in place today. Used for housing during the period in the 1950s when H. Rodney Sharp was restoring the Corbit-Sharp House, seen on the right, it is now a private home. At one time, the basement was used as the town jail.

The proud steeple of Immanuel Episcopal Church, Historic New Castle's most high profile structure, reaches to the pure blue of a spring sky. Built in 1703, it was the first parish of the Church of England in Delaware. A fire in 1980 burned all but the walls, which were used in its reconstruction. Many of Delaware's important historical figures—governors, senators and signers of the Constitution among them—are buried in the cemetery next to the church. New Castle, founded as a Dutch fort in 1651, became the capital of the colony in 1704 and the capital of Delaware State in 1776. Old Library Museum on Third Street was the second home of the New Castle Library. Designed by William Eyre, the 1892 hexagonal building includes a series of skylights and light-sinks which provide a bright interior and basement. Today it is used for special temporary exhibitions of New Castle and Delaware history.

The Butcher, The Baker, The Aeroplane Maker:
Business in New Castle, 1875-1950

◄ One of New Castle's most popular sights, the stately George Read House.

The 240 acres of history at Hagley, the original du Pont mills, estate, and gardens, invite people to walk back in time to the beginnings of the DuPont Company and to American life at home and at work in the 19th century. This is where in 1802 Eleuthere Irenee du Pont de Nemours established his black powder mills. The French emigre was among the first entrepreneurs to recognize the value of Delaware's location. The Henry Clay Mill (above), built as a cotton-spinning factory in 1814, today houses Hagley Museum's orientation center and some exhibition space. The DuPont Company took it over in the 1880s and converted it into a metal keg factory. Breck's Mill and Walker's Mill, (left) built between 1813 and 1815, originally made cotton and woolen goods. Today the mills are preserved as part of Hagley Museum and Library just upstream on the Brandywine River. Breck's Mill has been restored into stylish space for two art galleries.

The Brandywine River flows by Hagley Museum's stone mills and waterwheel evoking memories of the days when waterpower was the source of energy. Millstreams at Hagley still channel water to operate machinery. Here visitors can enjoy a unique glimpse into America's industrial past, especially the economic and technological expansion of the Brandywine region.

Delicate pink and white dogwood blossoms contrast with the sturdy stone mills that are part of the guided tours offered by Hagley Museum. Also included are the first du Pont family home and garden in America, a charming Georgian-style mansion with French-style gardens, where five generations lived.

Showy rhododendrons welcome spring to the acres of beautiful gardens that surround Rockwood Museum in Wilmington. Inspired by an English country house, this excellent example of Rural Gothic architecture was built in 1851 by merchant-banker Joseph Shipley. Its rooms are filled with American, English and continental decorative arts spanning the 1600s to the 1800s.

The Delaware History Center's period archway over Market Street Mall points to the Old Town Hall Museum, used occasionally for exhibitions and special events. Also included in the Historical Society of Delaware's complex are its Library, the Delaware History Museum in a restored F.W. Woolworth's store and Willingtown Square, a park with six late 18th and early 19th century houses that were moved there. ▶

Snow brings an air of serenity to Henry Francis du Pont's monument to the American decorative arts from 1640 to 1840, the main museum at Winterthur Museum, Garden & Library. In it are 175 rooms with period settings that celebrate the creative genius of furniture makers, silversmiths, painters and other craftsmen.

The busy Amtrak station in downtown Wilmington, built in 1905 and restored in 1984, keeps a dignified foot in the past while all around it progress brings sleek high-rises like the First USA building that is part of the Christina Gateway.

The Delaware Art Museum in Wilmington, the state's premier fine arts institution, is home to America's finest collection of Pre-Raphaelite art (above). The artistic heritage of the Brandywine Valley began here in 1912 with a collection of works by illustrator Howard Pyle, the heart of the museum's unrivaled collection of American illustration. Acclaimed collections of 19th and 20th century American art include works by Edward Hopper, John Sloan, Winslow Homer and three generations of Wyeths. The Delaware Art Museum offers a regular schedule of traveling exhibitions from leading museums throughout the world. Its Biennial (above right) is a juried exhibition with contemporary works by artists from throughout the Mid-Atlantic region. The Sewell C. Biggs Museum of American Art in Dover (right) houses a personal collection of paintings, furniture and silver that has been in the making for more than 50 years and surveys major periods in American art.

Rockford Park in Wilmington glows with the vibrant colors of fall which frame Rockford Tower, a distinctive landmark since it was completed in 1901. Built with Brandywine granite, the 75-foot-high, Italian Renaissance-style tower still supplies water to the city of Wilmington.

Commuters cheered in December 1995 when the Delaware 1 bridge spanning the Chesapeake and Delaware Canal opened. It is located just west of St. Georges Bridge, which had carried the burden of north-south traffic on Route 13 since 1942. Every day, about 40,000 vehicles cross the new six-lane cable bridge supported with 336-foot high columns on either bank.

The day ends softly and gloriously over the Chesapeake and Delaware Canal, which runs for 13.6 miles from the Chesapeake Bay to the Delaware River. Constructed between 1824 and 1829, it is one of the country's most important canals and is owned and managed by the United States Army Corps of Engineers.

Under moonlight or sunlight, the volume of traffic crossing the Delaware Memorial Bridge has sped along steadily since its first span opened in 1951. Daily traffic on the twin spans runs at about 85,000 vehicles or some 31 million per year. ▶

The trees say it's back-to-school time at the one-room Octagonal School near Leipsic, but any children's voices heard coming from within would indicate a field trip is in progress and not that class is in session. Built in 1831, the school is a museum today.

Recess means high-spirited fun for Amish children who attend classes in their simple white schoolhouse west of Dover. Bars to climb and swings to ride invite them to make the most of their outdoor break from the classroom.

One of Milford's historic gems, the Parson Thorne Mansion has a colorful history. Built in the 1730s, it progressed from settler's dwelling to Georgian and then to Victorian in style. Located on the Mispillion River, Milford is half in Kent County and half in Sussex.

Phillip Barratt built this chapel in 1780 for the Methodist Society, then a part of the Anglican/Episcopal church. Just four years later the chapel served as the site for a meeting to establish the Methodist Episcopal Church. Thus Barratt's Chapel, located north of Frederica, is known as "the cradle of Methodism" in America. Today it is a Museum open to the public on weekend afternoons.

Snow dusts some of the historic buildings that are part of the Delaware Agricultural Museum in Dover, where visitors can explore 200 years of farm life in the First State.

Old Christ Church in Laurel, built in 1771, is open Sundays during the summer allowing visitors a look at its handsome unpainted heart-of-pine interior.

The spirit of the season warms the cold white of winter at the New Castle-Frenchtown Railroad Ticket Office. Constructed in 1832, it occupied several locations before being placed here in New Castle's Battery Park in the 1950s. The New Castle-Frenchtown route initially connected the Delaware River with the Elk River, which flows into the Chesapeake Bay. A toll road was developed here in the 1780s, and by the 1820s a rail line was laid. This rail traffic was pulled by horse until a steam engine was purchased from Great Britain in 1832.

Chateau Country in northern New Castle County

The Land

The second smallest state in the United States, Delaware is 96 miles long and varies from 9 to 35 miles wide. None other than Thomas Jefferson recognized that in this case, size does not count. He named it the "Diamond State for being a small jewel with many facets." The name still applies.

One transplanted Chicagoan, experiencing her first Spring in the First State, marveled at the abundance of blossoming trees and plants and says she uses one word to describe the season to friends back home: "Pink." Equally charming is Fall, when trees glow with colors so warm they could give Vermont a run for its money. Snowfalls are few, but often are effective in adding a layer of enchantment to nature. The dog days of August bring wet-blanket levels of humidity, but the good news is that the sea breezes are never far away.

In gently rolling hills in northern Delaware, cows graze in pastures not far from elegant estates which prompted the "Chateau Country" sobriquet. Extensive areas of environmentally valuable wetlands host millions of migrating birds and tens of thousands of birdwatchers, in no particular order. Outstanding among these are Bombay Hook National Wildlife Refuge east of Smyrna and the Prime Hook National Wildlife Refuge, northeast of Milton. Elevations in Delaware range from sea level to 442 feet atop an unnamed hill near Ebright Road in northern New Castle County. The twin-spanned Delaware Memorial Bridge's elevation is comparable.

About 30 percent of Delaware is forested, with oak and pine forests predominating in the coastal plain and oak and tulip tree forests most common in the state's northern tip, which lies in the Piedmont Plateau region. A dozen state parks offer trails for hiking and horsebacking, facilities for camping, ponds for boating, inland bays for surf casting, shores for crabbing and clamming, and endless opportunities for feasting on the joys of nature. Among them are Delaware Seashore State Park, a narrow, six-mile-long spit of land separating the Atlantic Ocean from Rehoboth Bay, and White Clay Creek State Park north of Newark, part of a preserve that extends into Pennsylvania and offers lush greenery and rushing streams.

Because of its location in a transition zone, the White Clay Creek watershed is home to some unusual plants and animals. Some varieties are at the northern limit of their range, others at the southern limits. The river meanders for about eight miles, in most places kept cool by a forest canopy. This section of the river's main stem is close to the Pennsylvania border.

A Monarch butterfly pauses and poses amid the beauty of Prime Hook National Wildlife Refuge, northeast of Milton. The refuge was established in 1963 to protect coastal wetlands, where waterfowl such as Canada geese, black ducks, mallards and wood ducks make their homes. The area has more than 15 miles of creeks perfect for kayaking and canoeing.

The Primula Garden at Winterthur Museum, Garden & Library reaches its glorious prime on schedule, part of a well-orchestrated succession of bloom that delights visitors from late January to December.

Two magnificent flowering dogwoods in New Castle, once the state's Colonial capital, exemplify the glories of spring in Delaware.

When vacationers tire of the sandy beaches along Delaware's coastline, they can do some rock hopping at Port Mahon on the Delaware Bay.

◄ A patch of woodlands at Winterthur Museum, Garden & Library merely hint at the horticultural genius of Henry Francis du Pont. He nurtured the 940-acre property for more than 65 years, selecting the choicest plants from around the world to create a matchless naturalistic garden.

Sunset approaches near Augustine Beach as a lone heron stands overshadowed by the invasive phragmites that are taking over the wetlands and creating problems in Delaware marshes.

The ever-charming Brandywine Creek goes
with the flow, looking upstream from the
waterfall near Breck's Mill to the Tyler
McConnell Bridge.

A sweep of yellow rocket, related to the mustard plant, covers an open field with glory in the White Clay Creek State Park.

Some grazing cattle enjoy lunch in a field near Corner Ketch, a community that has been part of a housing boom in the Hockessin area throughout the 1980s and '90s.

Looking like some creature from Star Wars, an irrigation system rests in the glow of a golden sunset on a farm near Middletown.

They're getting rarer, but one can still enjoy pastoral scenes like this of Belted Galloways grazing on a farm near Route 15 in Middletown.

Near Brandywine Creek State Park in northern Delaware, off Route 100, a rainbow salutes the sturdy oak that has stood there for decades. ▶

A morning mist subdues the riotous colors of fall at a neatly kept farm near Hoopes Reservoir in New Castle County.

One is not a lonely number when you're a swan in a pond taking in the autumn-tinged glory of Winterthur Museum, Garden & Library. The gazebo, known as Bristol Summer House, distinguishes this patch of beauty among the 940 acres that comprise Winterthur.

The water tower at Granogue, a du Pont family estate built in 1923 near Centreville, peeks out at the panoply of fall colors brightening its rolling countryside.

The ongoing fascination with the Amish is fueled by scenes like this displaying their artistic touch in assembling cornstalks to be gathered.

The northernmost stand of bald cypress trees in North America can be found at Trussum's Pond near Laurel. Nature photographers can't get enough of these magnificent trees with knobby joints standing in crystal clear black water. ▶

Vermont's reputation as the premier place to see foliage could be threatened by golden panoramas like this one near Delaware City.

Subdued lighting fails to dim the warmth of fall at Bombay Hook National Wildlife Refuge. Auto tour routes and walking paths lead to observation trails and towers on the 15,122-acre site.

A pond on this farm near Route 100 in northern Delaware mirrors the pretty sky, the white barn and fence and the fall-colored trees. ▶

Impressionistic reflections of fall on the Brandywine Creek near the DuPont Experimental Station overshadow two white ducks who are leaving the scene of beauty.

On a clear autumn day, maple and oak trees along the Brandywine River wear the finest colors of the season.

Ducks swoop and skim over the gold-kissed marshlands at Bombay Hook National Wildlife Refuge.

The interaction of morning fog and a golden sunrise creates a magical landscape in the area of Reedy Point Bridge in New Castle County.

A coating of ice so artistically transforms the trees at Lums Pond that the scene looks more like a painting than a photograph.

The bright whiteness of snow brings out the blackness of this creek near Rockwood Museum and Trussum Pond (left) with its distinctive bald cypress trees.

On Amish farms west of Dover, winter's harshness makes the going harder for a buggy and the grazing less enjoyable for two horses.

Seashore

Delaware's 25 miles of coastline pack in every seashore delight one can imagine. Small-town charm and big-city personalities. Orangey sunrises on the ocean side and purple-tinged sunsets over the bay. Expansive state parks with beautiful beaches and beautiful beaches with high-spirited boardwalks. Boardwalk stores selling kitschy knickknacks with seashell motifs and chic boutiques with racks of the most *au courant* fashions. A good place for bird watchers and paradise for people watchers. Early-morning surf fishing and wee-hours nightclub hopping. Kids making sandcastles and adults making reservations for dinner at the newest hot spot. Well-preserved historic sites and well-oiled arcade games.

Laid-back Lewes, the northernmost community and gateway to Delaware's seashore, abounds in historic attractions that include Shipcarpenter Square, an enclave of private homes dating from 1720 to 1880; the charming Zwaanendael Museum, which celebrates 300-plus years of Dutch History; and the Historic Complex, which includes the Lightship Overfalls Museum.

High-profile Rehoboth Beach, the main attraction with its wide beaches and mile-long boardwalk, draws sun-seekers by the hundreds of thousands every summer. So many come from Washington, D.C., that it's known as the "Nation's Summer Capital." Its name came from the Biblical term meaning "room enough," which applies most of the time, but not in the height of summer when you're waiting in line for some hot beach fries or for a table at one of the town's sophisticated restaurants.

Uninhibited Dewey Beach is a sandbar community that can boast of an ocean on one side of the street and a bay on the other. It's a haven for young professionals, who play hard during the day skimboarding, jet skiing and catamaran sailing, and party hard during the night at numerous nightclubs. Named after a hero of the Spanish-American War, Dewey is one of Delaware's youngest incorporated communities.

The "Quiet Resorts" of Bethany Beach and Fenwick Island have held on to their small-town charm, carefully managing commercial growth and maintaining their miles of uncrowded beaches, broad bays and wildlife preserves. Many of these delights are in the area's three state parks offering outstanding fishing and boating. And the Fenwick Island Lighthouse, built in 1858, stands tall as a distinctive landmark.

Sand and sky blush in Fenwick Island as another sunset casts its magic spell.

◄ A tangle of snow fence and beach grass south of Cape Henlopen State Park points to the World War II lookout tower that has long been a welcome sight for beach lovers. Cape Henlopen is part of parkland owned by the state and federal governments that covers more than half of Delaware's 25-mile long Atlantic coastline.

Looking east at sunset in Assawoman Wildlife Refuge, a dramatic sky-scape creates an ideal backdrop for the majestic silhouettes of native pine trees.

Graceful egrets evoke visions of Swan Lake ballerinas as they feed in the waters of Derrickson's Creek near Fenwick Island. ▶

Sunset paints the sand pink for a few brief moments at Cape Henlopen State Park, the state's most-visited park. Its number of visitors has tripled since the early 1990s to almost one million annually.

◀ A fiery sunrise at Indian River Inlet cheers the early risers who believe the best way to start the day is to go fishing.

The rising sun puts on a spectacular show
for riders on the Cape May Lewes Ferry as
they approach the Henlopen Lighthouse.

At Fenwick Island, footprints in the sand have a short but oh-so-sweet life.

The main event along the Delaware coastline looks particularly appealing with its wash of pink.

The craggy personality of a speciman driftwood punctuates the hush of an early morning sunrise at Fenwick Island.

A relatively rare sight at the shore, snow spreads a coat of white over the undulating dunes in Rehoboth Beach and at Cape Henlopen State Park, where a snowy road leads to a distinctive landmark. This former World War II spotting tower is one of several that can be seen along Delaware's shoreline. Today, the curious can climb to the top when it is open (during State Park hours in the summer) and on a clear day, can see Cape May, New Jersey.

Soft shadows created by a gentle sunset create mysterious patterns on a sand dune at South Bethany Beach.

A sandy dune near Cape Henlopen State Park invites walkers to follow in the footsteps of other nature lovers.

A many-splendored sunrise at Bethany Beach joins sea and sky in a riot of color that celebrates the new day. ▶

A seagull soars over Delaware Seashore State Park, which offers seven miles of oceanfront splendor with parklands that extend west to Rehoboth Bay.

Where most see intriguing patterns created by beach grass, environmentalists respect its vital role in maintaining and stabilizing sand dunes. ▶

Conch shells dot the beach north of Fenwick Island, left there by a storm that rearranged the elements of the ocean floor.

The occasional nor'easter sends crashing waves that can threaten the makeup of Delaware's wide beaches, but sand replenishment helps repair the damage.

Layers of sunset hopscotch across Indian River Inlet to Burton's Island, an area that birdwatchers favor for its abundant waterfowl, wading birds and songbirds.

A bird's-eye view of Assawoman Bay shows how the tide has worked its artistry while clammers poke around in the shallow water.

A lone fisherman basks in the solitude of Indian River Inlet as gentle waves lap the shore.

The peaceful beauty of Assawoman Wildlife Area, tucked away on the back bays of Southern Delaware, creates Rorshach-like patterns that need no interpretation. Its 2,000 acres of marsh, fields and forest are populated with native wildlife. ▶

A windsurfer zooms along at the speed of light in Rehoboth Bay.

Photographic creativity combines two sunsets over Rehoboth Beach, doubling the pleasure and giving clouds a golden lining.

Snow accentuates the wide variety of plants and trees found on the bay side of South Bethany.

Cloud-like sprays of water whipped up by a heavy surf at Indian River Inlet look like they belong in the sky.

Beach grass grows abundantly on a dune north of Bethany Beach overlooking a scene of pure pleasure: gentle surf, pink sunset and the opportunity to fish. ▶

University of Delaware Football

People, Places & Events

Whether they want to dip their toes in the ocean or applaud a first-class Broadway show, savor down-home treats at an ethnic festival or cheer and yell at a NASCAR race, Delawareans have a major advantage. Getting there is a breeze because "there" is never very far away. The state's diminutive size pays off for its approximately 772,000 residents who enjoy short commutes between office and golf course, and between home and world-class museums. And when big-city attractions beckon, they're not far away either. Easy day-trip options include Philadelphia and Baltimore, New York and Washington, D.C.

During some times of the year, only the most culturally needy leave the state because there's so much going on at home. Take spring, for example. There's Wilmington Flower Market in Rockford Park, a long-established fund-raiser for children's agencies with carnival rides, nifty boutiques and plants to please every gardener in town; Historic Old Dover Days, complete with the centuries-old tradition of dancing around the Maypole; the chi-chi Point-to-Point steeplechase races at Winterthur that bring out more than 20,000 people; the nationally televised McDonald's LPGA Championship, which attracts close to 100,000 people; and the roaring NASCAR races at Dover Downs where some 110,000 people jam the grandstand every race day.

Spring also brings a variety of tasty ethnic festivals, the spiciest and biggest being St. Anthony's Italian festival; the ever-expanding Clifford Brown Jazz Festival; and Separation Day, which attracts 10,000 to New Castle to celebrate Delaware's separation from Pennsylvania and England.

In between, there are Blue Rocks baseball games, Wizards and Genies soccer matches, parades and parties. In 1998, Delawareans gathered by the thousands for the commissioning of the *Kalmar Nyckel,* the authentically reconstructed tall ship that is a replica of the one that in 1638 brought Swedes to Wilmington as the first European settlers.

Come summer, First Staters find the the lure of the beach irresistible, and more and more that attraction extends to the "shoulder seasons" of spring and fall. And they keep getting broader as word of their charm spreads.

All contribute to making the First State first rate.

For years, they've done it every month, November through March, just for the chill of it. But in February 1998, the Lewes Polar Bear Club plunged into the icy waters at the beach to benefit the Special Olympics. Anyone is welcome to join them. Just show up at 1 p.m. at Cape Henlopen State Park on the first Sunday of the month, except for January when it's on New Year's Day.

Rockford Park's distinctive water tower has seen a lot of Flower Markets and a lot of people having a good time at the annual fund-raiser checking out boutiques, playing games, munching on pizza and funnel cakes and shopping for flowers and plants.

Kids gleefully spin and turn and whiz by on the carnival-style rides at Flower Market, an annual rite of spring in Wilmington since 1921. Proceeds from the high-spirited outdoor event benefit children's agencies.

One of the Delaware's grandest events, Winterthur's Point to Point attracts some 20,000 people each May. As always, the new-money crowd, many of them bankers socializing in tents, rub shoulders with old-money regulars parked in full view of the finish line. The Antique Carriage Parade, with its magnificent horses and variety of surreys, wagons and carriages, some spectacular and carrying splendidly dressed people, makes it clear this is no ordinary horse race. Point-to-Point is the quintessential people-watching event, but most come to cheer the amateur steeplechase racing.

◀ Point to Point

Since it started 20 years ago, organizers have added more and more events to please the crowd — a tailgating competition, dog-jumping competition, pony rides for kids and the appearance of the renowned Budweiser Clydesdale horses.

The DuPont Country Club shows off its natural splendor for both golfers and fans at a jewel of the Ladies Professional Golf Association, the $1.3 million McDonald's Championship.

The McDonald's LPGA Championship in May 1998 attracted more than 2,500 volunteers who helped raise a record $2 million for Ronald McDonald House Charities.

The best women golfers play at the
McDonald's LPGA, one reason why more
than 100,000 people came to watch
during the seven-day event.

Visitors wandered through some 15 homes and 30 gardens that were open for tours during a day in Old New Castle, the town where William Penn first landed in 1682.

At a Day in Old New Castle, a fife and drum corps competed with the clip-clopping of horse-drawn carriages for the most historic sounds. William Penn was there. In costume. And so was his personal secretary. They strolled the streets during the 74th anniversary celebration of the town's historic beginnings. New Castle remains today much as it was in colonial days, with more than 20 historic sites dating back to 1655.

Civil War Re-enactments at Brandywine Creek State Park on Memorial Day weekend drew large crowds of people who watched living-history battles such as Manassas played out. By re-enacting Civil War battles, participants get an up-close and personal history lesson. The weekend-long activities at Brandywine Creek State Park benefitted the Fort Delaware Society.

Crowds jammed Rodney Square for the super-successful and ever-growing Clifford Brown Jazz Festival sponsored by the City of Wilmington.

The handsome *Kalmar Nyckel* comes through the C&D Canal on its way back from a six-week maiden voyage to its base at the Kalmar Nyckel Shipyard and Museum in Wilmington. This is a modern-day replica of the ship that brought Swedes to Delaware in 1638. They established a colony in Wilmington that was not only the first permanent settlement in Delaware but in North America. Since it was launched in 1997, Delaware's Tall Ship has assumed a high profile in the First State and at various festivals in Baltimore, Philadelphia and Norfolk.

Competitors in the Christiana Care Cup, part of the First Union Cycling Festival, catch a fleeting glimpse of the scenic Hoopes Reservoir in northern New Castle County.

The loveliness of spring in Delaware is designed for garden tours, many of which are fund-raisers. Among them are the Lewes Garden Tour (left) and Wilmington Garden Day, when Mount Cuba inevitably shines as a favored stop.

Dover reverberates with the roar of the NASCAR races one weekend every spring and fall. Crowds exceeding 110,000 piled into Dover Downs International Speedway in May for one of the Winston Cup series' premier races, the MBNA Platinum 400. Above is racer Bill Elliott during the qualifying races.

Jeff Gordon, the Winston Cup points leader, has had three wins in 10 starts at Dover Downs' famous Monster Mile.

Wilmingtonians love their Blue Rocks and Frawley stadium where the championship team plays with the city skyline as a backdrop. The Kansas City Royals minor league team keeps fans coming back for good baseball, like a successful slide into second base, and the high-spirited entertainment. Between innings, there's always some kind of diversion pitched out to the crowd, from singing and dancing to ball-throwing contests and special performances such as "Rockin' Ray" Masel and his sidekick, Skyy Dog.

The explosion of soccer leagues for kids throughout the state during the 1980s inevitably led to professional teams like the Delaware Wizards, a professional men's team, and the Delaware Genies, a women's soccer team that will become professional in the year 2000. Both compete in the Mid-Atlantic Division of the USISL (United Systems of Independent Soccer Leagues). High school girls' soccer has been identified as the fastest-growing sport for women.

The Irish, who've been in Delaware longer than the du Ponts, wear their green with a powerful dose of pride during the colorful St. Patrick's Day Parade in Wilmington. A happy dog and his master ride in their shamrock-festooned truck, and marching bands add a musical beat. The "Family Boardwalk" (below) bring their own brand of independence to the annual 4th of July parade in Bethany Beach.

Fort Delaware State Park on Pea Patch Island in the Delaware River near Delaware City was originally built as a fort during the Civil War but then turned into a prisoner-of-war camp.

Living History presentations at Fort Delaware State Park feature characters such as General Schoepf, commander of the prisoner-of-war camp, ably played by historian Dale Fetzer.

As ethnic festivals go, St. Anthony's Italian Festival outdoes them all. This colorful, week-long party draws huge crowds to Little Italy for everything from Old World food and religion to the latest in scary rides and popular performers. From the front of St. Anthony's church, passsersby can catch a glimpse of a high-wire motorcycle act, (right) which pretty much tells it all, if you add wonderful aromas of hearty Italian food.

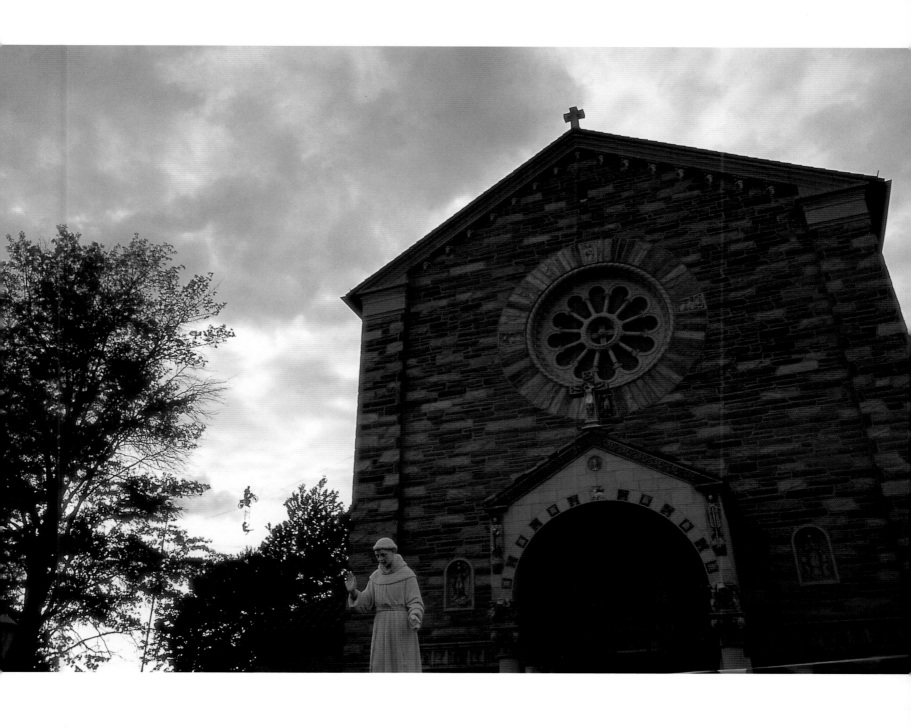

Whether jumping waves or surfing, beach-goers delight in the brilliant surf at Indian River Inlet.

◀ Colorful sailboats dot the gray Delaware River in races off Battery Park
   in New Castle.

High-energy volleyball contests go non-stop at Delaware's beaches. Here the action takes place on the bay side of Dewey Beach.

Walkers, bicyclers and daydreamers create a tableau of outdoor pleasures in Battery Park along the Delaware River in New Castle.

The sun does its Midas thing, spreading a lustrous glow over Rehoboth Bay where windsurfers play.

Many First Staters believe that in order to be a true-blue Delawarean, you must attend University of Delaware football games. Tailgating is de rigueur, but more important is cheering on those Fightin' Blue Hens, consistently ranked among the nation's top 20 Division I-AA colleges. Their popular coach, Tubby Raymond, is recognized throughout the country as one of college football's best. For generating school spirit, the University of Delaware marching band ranks right up there with the football team

The fiery colors of autumn are subdued by the morning mist as a fisherman tries his luck at Beck's Pond near Glasgow.

Swirling soft mists at Lums Pond near the C&D Canal enhance the serenity of an early-morning fishing expedition.

Of the millions of birds that stop by the Bombay Hook National Wildlife Refuge, no species is more abundant than snow geese. During one count on a given day in early spring, there were 198,000 of the migrating water fowl enjoying a little R&R.

The Nanticoke Indians who live just west of the Indian River Bay in Sussex County go about their everyday business in the same fashion as their neighbors. But they've never forgotten their past and still meet together as a tribe and hold ceremonies for which they dress and perform just as their ancestors. Every fall, thousands come to the Nanticoke Indian Powwow in Millsboro for two days of ceremonial drumming, dancing, storytelling, and Indian crafts and food. More than 45 different Indian tribes come from throughout the country to join the Nanticoke for this festive event.

Return Day, always held two days after a presidential election in the Courthouse Circle in Georgetown, is uniquely Delawarean. No other state has such a celebration, which is a carry-over from an era when people had to travel to the county seat to hear election news. Winning and losing candidates, who come from all over the state, ride with their opponents in horse-drawn carriages in a parade through town. The high-spirited hoopla includes the ceremonial burying of a hatchet. Everyone has a good time, but the winners invariably have more fun than the losers.

The University of Delaware basketball team, also known as the Blue Hens, has made its home state proud with some trips to the NCAA tournaments. Here, the team plays at the university's new Bob Carpenter Center in the final game of the America East tournament. The state bird, the Blue Hen chicken, is the source of the nickname for UD's teams. It recognizes the spirit of Delaware's Revolutionary War troops, who were called "Blue Hen's Chickens" for fighting with the same tenacity as the feisty, blue-tinted game cocks they carried with them.

When the occasional snowstorm invites Delawareans out for some winter fun, they dust off their sleds for a slide or two at Brandywine Creek State Park (above), Rockford Park (lower left) and even Cape Henlopen State Park on sand dunes more accustomed to bare feet than to sled runners. The enthusiasm of the sledders makes up for the gentleness of the inclines.

The quality and variety of

Delaware's businesses

has helped the state earn a

national reputation as

an economic powerhouse.

Partners in Progress

Delaware State Chamber of Commerce

Origins of the Delaware State Chamber of Commerce date back to 1837, when prominent local businessmen formed the Wilmington Board of Trade "for the better organization and regulation of the trade and business of Wilmington, mercantile, manufacturing and mechanic." At that time, Wilmington was a manufacturing hub, producing railroad cars, wheels, and sailing ships, as well as gunpowder and dynamite at the DuPont Company Powder Works.

Today, the state's manufacturing climate still ranks high. A 1998 *Industry Week* magazine study of 315 metropolitan statistical areas ranked the Wilmington/Newark area third in terms of manufacturing strength and first in the country for workforce productivity.

The first Board of Trade focused mainly on the development of the city's waterfront, which is still a major concern. The group lost momentum after its first two years, surged in a brief comeback during the late forties, but went dormant in December of 1853. It was not until 1867 that a young Quaker businessman, Joshua T. Heald, brought the Board of Trade back to life "to promote unity of action, and to cultivate a more intimate and friendly acquaintance among the business men of the City."

The beginning of the Twentieth Century brought more interest in the Board and its activities. Records show that in 1901, the Board had a mere 164 members, a number that increased to 938 in 1914. During this time, the Board addressed issues such as road improvements, child labor laws, interstate tariff rates, city parkland acquisitions, and trade training in public high schools.

In May of 1912, the Board decided to join the National Chamber of Commerce, dropping its affiliation with the National Board of Trade, and shortly thereafter became the Chamber of Commerce, Wilmington. Membership began to soar, and Josiah Marvel, a local attorney, was elected as the first president of the Chamber the following year. Under Marvel's leadership, the Chamber became a well-respected voice for business. Marvel was presented with a trophy in recognition of his strong leadership, and today his legacy lives on in the presentation of the annual Marvel Cup award to a member of the community who exemplifies Marvel's attributes in performance and community service.

The Chamber of Commerce, Wilmington, often took on issues that reached farther than the boundaries of the City of Wilmington, and legally changed its name to Chamber of Commerce, Delaware, Inc. in 1942. In 1953, when the organization officially assumed a statewide focus, it became the Delaware State Chamber of Commerce.

While influential, the State Chamber remained small, and until 1979, membership lingered at around 500. Today under the leadership of President John M. Burris, the Delaware State Chamber of Commerce is considered the First State's largest business advocacy organization offering a variety of benefits, services, training programs and marketing opportunities to its 3,400 members. The Chamber is also one of seven chambers in the nation that is the National Association of Manufacturers' affiliate at the state level.

Throughout the '90s, Delaware has remained the premier corporate domicile—more than 50 percent of the Fortune 500 companies traded on the New York Stock Exchange are incorporated in Delaware, and the 1997 *Financial World* annual survey ranked Delaware as the second best state in the nation for its business climate in the following four categories: Cost of Doing Business, Current Affairs, Economic Potential and Educated Labor Supply. The State Chamber is one of many organizations that has contributed to Delaware's great success. The following represents, in a nutshell, what the Chamber is today, after more than 160 years of service to the business community.

Representing Legislative Interests

The State Chamber spends a significant amount of time and effort representing the legislative interests of the business community at the federal, state and local levels. Through its registered lobbyists, the Chamber's Government Relations department works to ensure that members' positions on key issues are effectively communicated.

State Chamber members play an important part in the Chamber's government relations efforts, providing support for the Chamber's lobbying efforts. Members also help shape policy by participating in committees dedicated to specific legislative concerns, such as employee relations and taxes.

Joining all of these elements together—Chamber committee members, Government Relations staff, and individual Chamber members—has created one of the most influential and effective political coalitions in the State of Delaware. This large force has been successful in handling a wide spectrum of issues ranging from personal income tax cuts to unemployment compensation, health care reform, gross receipts tax law changes and regulatory reform.

Communicating Important Information

The Chamber's first publication, the *News Bulletin,* was created in 1935 and contained facts, editorials, committee reports, and wrap-ups of National Chamber of Commerce news. The *Bulletin* evolved into a tabloid newspaper called the *State Chamber News* in 1981, a biweekly business news publication.

In 1994, the State Chamber created the *Business Journal,* an oversized monthly four-color magazine. Today the *Business Journal* is the only statewide monthly magazine of its kind in Delaware. The magazine includes statewide business news, business people who make the news and analysis of issues affecting the business community. With a readership of 30,000, the publication has been honored by such organizations as the Delaware Press Association, the National Federation of Press Women, and the Delaware Tourism Office.

Other State Chamber publications include the annual *Membership Directory*

One Commerce Center, located at 12th and Orange Streets in Wilmington, serves as headquarters for the Delaware State Chamber of Commerce. ▶

& Business Resource Guide, which lists all 3,400 Chamber members alphabetically as well as by business category; a *Legislative Roster,* with names, addresses and photographs of all state and local government officials; and *Monday Morning,* a weekly status report of bills introduced in the General Assembly.

Assisting Small Businesses

The Small Business Alliance is a volunteer-driven arm of the Delaware State Chamber of Commerce created in January of 1996 to serve the specific needs of member companies with 150 employees or fewer. Guided by its own 15-member Board of Managers, the Alliance strives to improve the competitive position of Delaware small businesses. The Alliance provides statewide leadership in legislative advocacy, cost-saving benefits and services, and cost-effective access to small business information, training and development programs, and networking opportunities. With 2,800 members statewide and growing, the Small Business Alliance is the largest small-business organization in Delaware.

Promoting Tourism

In May of 1996 the State Chamber took a big step forward in promoting tourism by opening the Visitors Center at Bridgeville, the most comprehensive information center in the state. The Center includes a life-size map of the East Coast, a Travel Board to aid visitors in selecting hotels and making on-the-spot reservations, a gift shop filled with popular Delaware souvenirs, and a newly developed Relocation Room showcasing Delaware realtors, designers and builders.

In its first two years of operation, the Visitors Center staff has served more than 56,000 people by providing information ranging from the traditional—hotel accommodations at the beach and great seafood restaurants—to the more unusual. The Delmarva Explorer™, with its touch-screen technology is the newest information display at the Visitors Center, a tremendous resource for information about the state and region.

Because of the dedication of staff and volunteers, the Visitors Center won the Governor's Tourism Award for the Best Welcome Center in both 1996 and 1997.

Recognizing Excellence in Education

The State Chamber's Superstars in Education program, which turns ten in 1999, honors innovative educational programs throughout the state and encourages replication of previous award-winning programs. Since its inception, Superstars has recognized over 100 exceptional programs from across the state.

A Selection Committee reviews and grades each nomination that is submitted and also makes site visits in order to select the most worthy programs. The Chamber holds an annual recognition dinner to honor the winners. But Superstars does more than praise the achievements of these individual programs for one day each year. Throughout the year, the Superstars in Education program supports many diverse educational efforts, such as Principal for a Day, which places business and government leaders in schools across the state to get a feel for what it's like to be a school principal for a day, and the new Kid Execs program that lets young people experience what

it's like to be in a CEO's shoes.

Also, in 1997, the State Chamber was able to help ten Delaware teachers pursue national certification, an expensive, time-consuming and exhaustive process that only a few exceptionally qualified and talented teachers are ever able to complete.

Providing Networking Opportunities

One of the main reasons people give for joining the State Chamber is the wide variety of networking opportunities, where members can meet business people from the local area as well as from across the state. The State Chamber offers more than 100 meetings and programs each year throughout the state including several networking breakfasts, a handful of early evening Mix & Market receptions, two legislative brunches each year, many informative seminars and conferences, as well as regular meetings of the State Chamber's 15 active committees throughout the year dealing with topics such as employee relations, taxes, education, the environment, technology and more.

Looking to the Future

As we approach the year 2000 and beyond, the Delaware State Chamber of Commerce will continue carrying out its ambitious mission—"To promote an economic climate that strengthens the competitiveness of Delaware businesses and benefits citizens of the state. The Chamber will provide services members want; it will serve and be recognized as the primary resource on matters affecting companies of all sizes; and it will be the leading advocate for business with government in Delaware."

The Visitors Center at Bridgeville was opened in May of 1996 by the State Chamber to help promote tourism statewide. ▶

Bell Atlantic

From the first telephone in Delaware in 1878 to the over five hundred thousand subscriber lines today, from the simple telephone service of a century ago to the sophisticated information-management network of today, the history of the telecommunications industry in the Diamond State has been marked by rapid growth and technological milestones. Bell Atlantic - Delaware, Inc. has been a vital part of that history since its incorporation in 1897. Formerly known as the Diamond State Telephone Company, it has been a member of the Bell Atlantic family of companies since 1984. It currently employs 1,100 people, with an annual payroll of over $40 million and pays thirty million dollars in Delaware taxes each year.

The firm has made a commitment to ensure that technological progress and outstanding customer service go hand-in-hand.

From its headquarters office at 901 Tatnall Street in Wilmington, Bell Atlantic has a significant presence in Delaware, providing its citizens with a vital public service, contributing to the economic well-being of the state, striving always to be an involved citizen of the community. It directs the most comprehensive, statewide fiber optic network in the nation. Delaware was one of the first states to convert totally from analog to digital switching. This continues a long tradition of firsts in America. Bell Atlantic was the first company to offer all of its customers access to their long-distance carriers, the first to offer statewide direct dialing capability, the first to deploy statewide computerized switching, and the first to offer a statewide Emergency 911 service.

Bell Atlantic - Delaware has been a pacesetter in installing fiber-optic cable in both the public network and in private networks for major customers.

Its network value is approaching $1 billion. In a fiber-optic system, tiny lasers convert voice and data communications into pulses of light that are carried on glass fibers thinner than human hair. The company has already deployed over 64,000 miles of fiber-optic cable throughout Delaware. Computer controlled switching machines allow Bell Atlantic to offer sophisticated services that meet the complex information-management needs of businesses as well as the growing needs of residential customers for services that make their lives simpler and easier.

The Bell Atlantic network's greatest strength is clearly that it is designed to grow, as customers' needs change.

The ability to expand the network with the latest technology, along with the skill and vision of the company's employees, enable Bell Atlantic to work in partnership with its customers to design custom solutions to new and evolving information-management needs. Today, Bell Atlantic does business in 13 states and the District of Columbia - and has operations and investments in 21 countries. Some 140,000 employees install and maintain over 40 million access lines and serve 5 million wireless customers worldwide. The resulting economies of scale provide the opportunity for lower cost for residential and business customers, as well as leading edge technology and a wide range of service choices for consumers.

The foundation of Bell Atlantic's relationship with its customers is not based on technology alone, however. It is built upon a long tradition of extraordinary customer care.

This spirit of service has been nurtured by generations of employees, and they display it both on and off the job. Through volunteer activities with a wide range of organizations, employees demonstrate their commitment to the communities in which they live. Their outside involvement varies from volunteering to work with handicapped children, to mentoring in our schools, to programs that benefit senior citizens. They are particularly supportive of education in Delaware and received the State's first "Partners In Education Award" from the Governor for their efforts. The strength of Bell Atlantic can be found in its people. This is never more apparent than during emergency conditions, like snowstorms, when employees have trudged many miles through snow to serve their customers. No matter the conditions, you will find the Bell Atlantic people on the job, keeping Delaware's telecommunications network functioning smoothly. Bell Atlantic is deeply committed to Delaware. Its high tech network has helped make the state an attractive place for businesses to locate, and the spirit of service of its employees has helped make Delaware an outstanding place to live.

Bell Atlantic - Delaware enters its second century with a broadened mission. It is no longer a telephone company but a telecommunications company that can move any kind of information, anytime, anywhere.

Delaware can continue to look to Bell Atlantic for quality service at competitive prices, and beyond that, support in its effort to maintain a strong economy, a decent order in society, the conservation of resources and an environment that enhances the quality of life. Bell Atlantic's history has been characterized by concern, not just for service, but for its customers, employees, stockholders and the Delaware communities, and this won't change. Carrying on Bell Atlantic's reputation for being a just, a thriving and a caring business through a second hundred years will be a fitting challenge for telephone people today and a fitting tribute to the pioneers who built this company with those qualities in mind.

THE
FUTURE
is
HERE.

EARLY.

For a preview of 21st century telecommunications, take a look at the state of Delaware today.

The Chase Manhattan Bank

Since opening its doors in Wilmington in 1982, Chase Manhattan Bank USA, N.A., has continued opening doors for Delawareans: to new employment opportunities, to the dream of home ownership and to a better quality of life for the communities it serves.

The first out-of-state credit card bank to move its headquarters to Delaware, Chase is now the state's 8th largest employer with more than 2,000 employees. Chase USA's credit card portfolio has more than 20 million accounts and over $30 billion in outstandings. Chase has relationships with more than 30 million consumers coast to coast.

But while credit card lending was the beginning for Chase USA in Delaware, the Bank has expanded its local operations to meet the needs of consumers here and around the country. Today, through its national consumer finance division located in Wilmington and Newark, Chase USA offers a variety of credit products, including credit cards, residential mortgages, auto loans, home equity loans and lines of credit, personal unsecured lines of credit and other secured consumer loans.

Chase USA is part of The Chase Manhattan Corporation, which has over $365 billion in assets. The Chase Manhattan Corporation provides integrated solutions that meet its customers' payment, savings, investment, insurance, credit and financial planning needs.

Chase also is committed to making life better, by improving the health and vitality of the communities it serves. Chase provides financial contributions and technical assistance to a variety of community organizations and through a broad volunteer program encourages, supports and rewards employees in their volunteer efforts. Chase also matches qualified employees' personal contributions through their extensive Matching Gift Program. In recognition of these efforts, Chase received the 1997 Points of Light Foundation "Award for Excellence in Corporate Community Service". One of the most prestigious awards in corporate volunteerism, it recognizes companies that have made an institutional commitment to employee volunteerism to help solve serious problems facing communities.

Chase USA's community development efforts have several components, which focus on key issues affecting Delaware and our society as a whole. Among Chase USA's key initiatives are those involving: affordable housing, economic development and social services for targeted areas; precollegiate and collegiate education, systematic school reform, training and employment. Chase helps create a marketplace of ideas, where policy issues are examined and nonprofits share information through increased networking capabilities, enabling them to improve their operational efficiencies.

Chase has actively pursued many innovative programs to the benefit of Delaware businesses and residents. It works with organizations to provide affordable housing opportunities, and offers an array of products to help first-time homebuyers realize their dreams of home ownership.

Chase USA also has focused on initiatives to improve the educational opportunities and welfare of Wilmington's children. Through the Chase Active Learning Program, educational grants were awarded to area middle schools in 1997 and 1998. This program is an initiative designed to support innovative instructional programs for middle grade students by engaging them in hands-on-discovery and experiential learning activities. The bank also partnered with Wilmington's Downtown Business Association to create and sponsor the "Halloween Hoot," a parade and festival for children providing a fun-filled day for families.

This commitment to the community — its present and its future — dates back to Chase's beginning in 1799 when its earliest predecessor, The Manhattan Company, was formed to supply New York with clean water to fight a yellow fever epidemic. The Bank of the Manhattan Company was founded simultaneously and in 1808, the City took over the water operation while the Bank of The Manhattan Company focused on providing personal banking services, flourishing in the process.

The Bank of The Manhattan Company began a tradition of innovative banking practices and by the mid and late 19th century, the bank had established itself as one of the largest holders of individual depositor accounts. At that time, the other part of Chase Manhattan — The Chase National Bank — had developed into a Wall Street powerhouse. By the time the two merged in 1955, The Bank of Manhattan operated 67 branches in New York City and was widely regarded as one of the most prestigious regional banks in America.

Under the leadership of David Rockefeller, The Chase Manhattan Bank became the largest bank in New York City. Rockefeller became chairman of the Bank in 1969, the same year The Chase Manhattan Corporation was formed and The Chase Manhattan Bank, N.A. became its wholly owned subsidiary.

Chase's leadership in the financial services industry continued and in 1981, when Delaware liberalized its banking laws to attract large bank holding companies to the state, Chase submitted its applications to open a banking subsidiary here. Its applications were approved and on February 2, 1982, The Chase Manhattan Bank (USA), N.A., opened its doors. Chase USA soon became a leading issuer of credit cards and other consumer products nationwide. Since 1995, when Chase merged with Chemical Banking Corporation to create the largest banking company in the United States, Chase USA has expanded further its consumer businesses and commitment to the Delaware community to better meet the needs of its customers nationwide and in Delaware — today and in the future.

Chase remains committed to helping consumers and businesses to achieve their financial goals. Chase will continue to capitalize on its strong brand name, superior information technology and effective partnerships to meet the challenges of the changing environment in Delaware — and around the globe — and continue to open new doors for employees, businesses and consumers.

Artesian Resources Corporation: Supplying Delaware's Water Needs

In 1905, when Aaron K. Taylor founded Artesian Resources Corporation (then Richardson Park Water Company), his concept of providing indoor plumbing and public water service to the working class was startling. Today, the company built on this visionary leadership continues to break new ground through exploration, innovation, and the development of a long-term, high quality water supply.

The largest investor-owned water utility in the state, Artesian serves 200,000 people in all three counties of Delaware—nearly 30 percent of the state's population as of December 31, 1997. The company's investment in new sources of water has been critical to economic development initiatives. Since 1992, Artesian has more than doubled its underground water supply, working aggressively to ensure that the company is able to keep pace with its growing customer base.

Early in 1998, Artesian announced plans to store 200 million gallons of water through a water management system known as Aquifer Storage and Recovery (ASR). The first such project in Delaware, ASR will enable Artesian to store excess water produced and treated during periods of low water consumption in a well drilled deep into a natural underground reservoir. During periods of higher consumption, the water stored through ASR can be recovered for customer use. When the ASR project is complete, Delaware will become one of only nine states in the country to use this outstanding in-ground water storage system.

While striving to expand its available water supply, Artesian has also worked closely with the Delaware Economic Development Office to enhance the business climate in Delaware by attracting desirable industries. Artesian strongly supports efforts that will bring good employers and high-quality jobs to the state. To meet the potential demand for wastewater services that new industries would create, a strategic partnership was established between Artesian Wastewater Management, Inc. (a wholly-owned subsidiary of Artesian Resources Corporation), George & Lynch, Inc. (a major regional heavy-construction contractor), and Woodward-Clyde International Americas (a subsidiary of URS Greiner, an international design and engineering firm). Organized as AquaStructure Delaware, L.L.C., the venture enables Artesian to provide a full range of water and wastewater management services.

By expanding its services, developing new water sources, adding new franchise territories, providing contract services to neighboring utilities and municipalities, and developing resources for high-water-use industries, Artesian has positioned itself to meet the long-term needs of both current and future customers. These strategic initiatives have also resulted in a strong financial performance. Traded on the NASDAQ National Market System since May 1996, Artesian Resources Corporation's stock has yielded both high demand and healthy returns. Recognizing the many factors that have contributed to this success, Artesian President and CEO Dian C. Taylor points to the continued importance of delivering superior customer service. "We are committed to going above and beyond to serve our customers," she says. "Although water utilities still operate as monopolies, we treat our customers as if they have a choice. It's the driving force behind everything we do."

Leaders in civic, environmental and business organizations, the people of Artesian are also committed to serving the communities in which they live and work. Many of the company's employees volunteer as mentors at an area school, while others participate in fund-raising activities for local charitable organizations. Artesian has also been involved in a number of environmental protection initiatives, including the annual Christina River Clean-up.

For more than 90 years, Artesian Resources Corporation has been driven by the mark of excellence set forth by Aaron K. Taylor and his son W. Howard Taylor, who presided over Artesian for more than 60 years. Providing quality water and superior service were guiding principles that W. Howard handed down to his sons, Norman and Ellis, and to his grandchildren and great-grandchildren. Throughout the company's history, the Artesian family has worked diligently to carry on the tradition of excellent service.

"Through sound management, water quality control and prudent infrastructure investment, Artesian has been able to supply our customers with the best-tasting, purest water," says Taylor. "We take pride in this fact, and support efforts designed to see that all customers are assured safe, quality drinking water."

Chicago-based FMC Corporation is one of the world's leading producers of chemicals and machinery for industry and agriculture, with sales of more than $4 billion and 100 production facilities and mines in 22 countries. The Fortune 150 company employs approximately 17,000 people worldwide.

The Pharmaceutical Division is headquartered in Philadelphia and is part of FMC's Specialty Chemicals Group. The Pharmaceutical Division's manufacturing is done at two ISO 9002 certified plants located in Newark, Delaware and Cork, Ireland. The Newark plant is located on Route 273/Ogletown Road. FMC's Pharmaceutical Division provides products, systems and technical customer services to the worldwide pharmaceutical industry, with a focus on new product development and applications research.

"Without the Newark plant and its team of people dedicated to producing products of the highest quality, we would not be in business." That comment from top corporate management in Chicago, underscores the Newark plant's key role in the multinational company's longstanding success. Every product manufactured and sold by the pharmaceutical division worldwide originates in Newark. The high-tech Newark plant occupies 27 acres. FMC has consistently reinvested in the Newark plant to maintain a leading edge, state of the art, world class facility over its 35 years of operation. More than 125 employees work at the plant, which features a computerized, enclosed, continuous process system that operates 24 hours a day. The plant utilizes a state-of-the-art automated packaging center, a warehouse, bright modern offices, and a separate coatings plant. A separate pilot plant is also on the property which enables FMC to provide customized technical services to help pharmaceutical and food manufacturing customers solve their key technical challenges. These efforts are supported by the division's research and development facility in Princeton, New Jersey, which is considered the best of its kind in the excipient supplier industry.

FMC is a global leading producer of binders and functional excipients for tablets, capsules and suspensions. The division's star product is Avicel® microcrystalline cellulose. Avicel® is a white, odorless, tasteless powder that is derived from purified alpha cellulose. Avicel® was discovered in the 1950's by the American Viscose Corporation in nearby Marcus Hook, Pennsylvania. The Newark plant started manufacturing the product in 1962. FMC became a part of the Newark community in 1963 when it purchased the American Viscose operations. Avicel® was originally introduced as a low-calorie food ingredient, but it was found to have potential use in pharmaceutical tablets. FMC's efforts to find multiple uses for the product have paid off handsomely with an expanded product line and significant market share.

Seventy-five percent of Avicel® sales are to pharmaceutical firms. In fact, virtually every major pharmaceutical company in the world uses Avicel® for at least one of its products. Its primary uses are as a binding agent for tablets and capsules, and as an aid to rapid disintegration of active drugs in the stomach. Avicel® is found in medications that treat cardiovascular disease, hypertension, diabetes, ulcers, and in over-the-counter pain relievers, cough and cold remedies, and vitamins.

Avicel® is also used throughout the food ingredients industry, because it is derived from the same type of cellulose found in many fruits and vegetables. Avicel® acts as a binder, thickener and stabilizer. It replaces fat and absorbs moisture in food products such as frozen desserts, salad dressings, nonfat yogurt, and pie fillings. Avicel® also helps maintain the taste, texture and "mouthfeel" of frozen desserts and lowfat products.

FMC expanded beyond the Newark plant when it built a plant in Cork, Ireland in 1978. Meanwhile, the Newark plant has expanded steadily to accommodate a growing product line. In the late 1970's and early 1980's a number of new pharmaceutical excipients were introduced.

Ac-Di-Sol® croscarmellose sodium is another cellulose-based product that is used to speed up the disintegration of tablets and capsules, resulting in faster drug action. An expansion occurred in 1985 to accommodate increased Ac-Di-Sol® production. Aqueous dispersion products came to market named Aquacoat® ECD ethylcellulose and Aquacoat® CPD cellulose acetate phthalate, along with Aquateric® aqueous enteric coatings. These are environmentally friendly, high-performance latex film coatings that modify the rate or target delivery of active drugs. They also mask bitter taste, and control the release of active ingredients, as in time release medication. The most recent Newark expansions occurred in 1987 when FMC opened its multi-million-dollar high-tech coatings plant to produce these products, and in 1993 an expansion for increased Avicel® production occurred.

Longevity and stability are hallmarks of the Newark site. Plant Manager David Del Carlo leads a seven-person management staff and an experienced team of employees who have accumulated more than 1,850 years of service and technical expertise. The plant's hourly employees are represented by the United Steel Workers of America, Local No. 13028. Labor-management relations have been characterized by a longtime record of freedom from labor strife. FMC Newark has historically scored high in safety. Plant management is also proud of its low rate of personnel turnover, which averages less than two percent per year.

FMC is committed to protecting the environment and the health and safety of its employees, their families and the public. For FMC, nothing is more important than keeping Newark safe. The plant's environmental equipment is operated and monitored 24 hours a day to protect air and water quality. FMC proudly supports and is a signatory to the Responsible Care® initiatives of the Chemical Manufacturers Association.

Greenwood Trust Company

Greenwood Trust Company was founded in 1911 in the idyllic Sussex County town which bears its name. Operating from a single retail location, the bank remained an independent fixture in Greenwood from its inception until the mid-1980's. In 1985 Greenwood Trust was purchased by Sears Roebuck and Co. to become a key part of their growing Sears Financial Network. Greenwood Trust was chosen by Sears to be the issuing bank for their new Discover Credit Card which was rolled out in early 1986.

In 1993 Greenwood Trust was spun off from Sears along with Dean Witter and Discover Card Services to become Dean Witter, Discover & Co. The following year Discover Card Services became NOVUS Services. May 1997 saw further exciting developments in the Greenwood Trust story, as Dean Witter, Discover & Co. merged with the Morgan Stanley Group to become one of the preeminent financial securities firms in the world. These new alliances were further consolidated in 1998 when the company's name was changed to Morgan Stanley, Dean Witter and Co. Greenwood Trust remains the primary issuer of credit cards of the NOVUS Network. In addition to issuing credit cards, the bank's retail facility offers a full array of consumer loans including residential construction, home purchase mortgages, home improvement loans, and secured and unsecured installment loans.

Today Greenwood Trust employs over 1700 employees in three Delaware locations. The largest of these facilities is the New Castle Operations Center situated in the New Castle Corporate Commons. This center is home to various support functions for the credit card business. Greenwood Trust's Newark facility, located on Chapman Road, houses New Accounts processing for the Discover Card and other NOVUS brands. The bank's retail facility and headquarters is located on West Market Street in Greenwood, though a new building is under construction for occupancy in late 1998.

Though it is a wholly owned subsidiary of Morgan Stanley Dean Witter, to most of their customers in and around Sussex and Kent Counties Greenwood Trust remains their familiar hometown bank. The bank is proactive in their approach to community reinvestment and supports a number of non-profit programs in the area. One initiative in particular that illustrates Greenwood Trust's philosophy towards its community is the Foundation Scholarship program. This scholarship was established by the bank to provide a tool to the community and its students to help build a successful future. Greenwood Trust strives to be not only a part of the community's financial sector, but a true neighbor to all of the community's citizens. This concept is best summed up in the slogan of Greenwood Trust's retail facility: "The Banking Services You Expect... The Friendliness You Appreciate." This personalized service and attention to individual needs has made Greenwood Trust Company a welcome friend and partner in the community.

Core values at Zeneca translate into social vision and volunteerism

In only a few short years, Fairfax-based **Zeneca Inc.** has rapidly risen to rank among the leaders of Delaware's business community, providing jobs for more than two thousand residents and contributing greatly to the overall health of the state's economy. But the greatest source of pride for this life sciences business isn't just the strong, bottom line numbers found in its annual report. It is also in the dedication to and the degree with which Zeneca supports the community at large through funding and active participation in programs that help enhance the quality of life here in Delaware and elsewhere.

Zeneca Inc. and its predecessor companies have been based in Delaware since the 1950s. One of Delaware's ten largest employers, Zeneca is engaged in the research, development, manufacture and marketing of ethical (prescription) pharmaceuticals, agricultural and specialty chemical products and the supply of health care services. Zeneca Inc. is a wholly owned subsidiary of Zeneca Group PLC, a major $8.6 billion international life sciences business based in London, England.

Throughout the United States, a total of 7,500 employees are employed by Zeneca. In Delaware, Zeneca has seven sites - all in New Castle County - with 2,600 employees. Approximately 750 of these employees work in research and development.

Social Responsibility at Zeneca

Zeneca and its employees have an outstanding tradition of supporting the community as volunteers and individual donors.

As the sole corporate sponsor of **REACH for Healthier Kids,** Zeneca recently provided a second, two-year, $100,000 grant to continue this unique mobile community outreach program aimed at families with pre-natal to pre-school children. Each week, the REACH van travels to five Wilmington and New Castle County communities to provide parents and caregivers with information to help ensure their children's health, nutrition, and well-being. *REACH for Healthier Kids* works in partnership with two large, nonprofit social service orga-

nizations: Children & Families First and The Family & Workplace Connection.

Through the **Adopt-a-School Collaboration,** an ever-expanding corps of more than 100 employee volunteers support P.S. duPont Elementary School near Zeneca's headquarters. This employee effort is enhancing the academic, social and interpersonal skills of some 1,300 students in grades four through six. Employee volunteers serve as mentors and HOSTS (Helping One Student To Succeed) tutors and Big Brothers or Big Sisters. A "Tech Team" of 20 employees is training teachers to use computers, many of which have been donated by Zeneca. The **Adopt-a-School Collaboration** is considered Zeneca's most comprehensive community outreach program and represents a long-term company commitment.

A charter member of Junior Achievement of Delaware, Zeneca provides funding, board leadership and volunteer support each semester. Zeneca volunteer teachers are involved at the elementary, junior high and senior high school levels to help students become workforce ready.

Zeneca makes an annual corporate donation to **Big Brothers/Big Sisters,** provides board leadership, and sponsors annually an internal bowl-a-thon, a major fund-raiser that has garnered strong employee participation. Zeneca volunteers also serve as Big Brothers or Big Sisters to individual children throughout the year.

Zeneca participates in other programs, which are not necessarily focused on children. As the founding sponsor of **National Breast Cancer Awareness Month,** Zeneca continues to support this effort, as well as the **A-Z Project** (mammograms for uninsured and underinsured Delaware women), **The Charter School of Wilmington,** the **Business/Public Education Council,** and **the arts**.

BioGrant is Zeneca's nationwide grant program that supports community-based nonprofit environmental projects in which Zeneca employees are personally involved as volunteers. Since

the grant program was launched in 1991, Zeneca has contributed half a million dollars to more than 100 nonprofit environmental projects in 16 states and four Canadian provinces.

Zeneca continues to support the national **Five-a-Day** For Better Health program that encourages Americans to eat five or more servings of fruits and vegetables every day.

More than 50 Delaware social service agencies are financially supported by Zeneca's annual employee **United Way of Delaware** campaign. Zeneca also provides a corporate donation.

Employees - and the company as a whole - also actively support a number of nonprofit activities and fundraisers such as the **American Heart Association Heart Walk,** the **Juvenile Diabetes Foundation Walk,** the **March of Dimes Walk-a-Thon, Meals on Wheels,** and **First Night Wilmington.**

Zeneca's community outreach work has earned it the designation, **"The Health Caring Company."** During 1998, Zeneca was officially commended by Delaware's House of Representatives for its community efforts; the company also received The Family & Workplace Connection's 1998 *Delaware Tomorrow Award* for its "extensive involvement with children's causes in the community." This award was also presented out of recognition of Zeneca's employee work/life commitment that includes the area's first sick child/elder care programs, dependent care referral services, on-site summer camps for children, on-site holiday child care and employee health and fitness programs. The latter includes on-site mammograms and health education and screenings for prostate cancer, hypertension, skin cancer and colorectal cancer.

"A dedication to excellence in each of our businesses isn't enough," says Zeneca Inc. Chairman A. Keith Willard. "We also have an obligation to serve the communities of which we are a part, and I am proud of the high degree to which this company and its employees have risen to meet that obligation."

Zeneca's community outreach logo - "THE HEALTH CARING COMPANY"- dramatizes the Company's philanthropic commitment to the communities in which it does business. ▶

ZENECA

THE HEALTH CARING COMPANY

M. Davis & Sons, Inc.

While headlines of the 1870s boasted about the formation of baseball's National League, Edward R. Davis found little time to enjoy the nation's new favorite pastime. Instead, Mr. Davis was spending many hours developing a small tinsmithing business that would evolve into the M. Davis & Sons, Inc. that is still part of Delaware today. Edward R. Davis was a Quaker from West Chester, Pennsylvania. A tinsmith by trade, he began operations at Lovering Avenue in Wilmington. Before buying a horse and wagon to facilitate his labor, he walked from house to house, carrying the tools and ladders needed to perform work on tin roofs, his primary product. Edward also spent his time repairing wash boilers, the copper tubs used to wash clothes on stovetops. In the early 1900s Edward built 1704 and 1706 Lincoln Street as a house, store and shop. His store sold cook stoves, kerosene stoves, warm air furnaces, oil lamps, smoke pipes and the associated hardware. At that time he employed approximately 30 men. Edward's principal customer was Bancroft Textile Mills. He crafted their oil cans, drip pans, and did some duct work. Edward Davis and his wife, Elizabeth, who had emigrated from Wales, had a son, Marcellus Davis, Sr. After his marriage in 1906, Marcellus rented his father's house at 1706 Lincoln Street. In 1912, Edward turned the business over to his son, the company's namesake, and moved to a farm near Coatesville, Pennsylvania. Marcellus Davis, Sr. operated his father's store until 1920, when he opened a wooden-floored shop in his basement. He concentrated his efforts on the textile mills, a local brewery, tin roofs, milk and ice cans and the installation of furnaces. A kind-hearted man, he assisted people who had fallen on hard times, often not charging at all for his services. The first vehicle in the M. Davis fleet was a Ford

Model T pick-up truck purchased by Marcellus, Sr. In 1931, having grown tired of life in the city, and wanting to experience country life, Marcellus moved to Silverside Road, and once again set up shop in the basement of his home. The Doeskin Paper Plant in Rockland became an M. Davis customer while the majority of the business stabilized. Marcellus Davis, Jr. more commonly known as 'Pete,' had begun working full-time for his father in 1930, but procured the business in 1946, upon the illness of Marcellus, Sr. He focused on paper mill work, as well as heating and air conditioning. Soon the DuPont Company became a customer and Pete's industrial contacts led to new opportunities in areas such as air and hood systems for the Exton Paper Company. M. Davis was incorporated in 1973, and moved into a shop on Lancaster Avenue. Today, Chairman Charles R. Davis, great-grandson of the founder, carries on the company's original mission to provide superior services at a fair price, guided by the philosophy that quality is never an accident - it is the result of attention to detail and a sincere effort by everyone involved. Four generations later, M. Davis & Sons, Inc. employs over 300 people from the Delmarva region and has grown to become one of Delaware Valley's leading providers of complete industrial and commercial contracting services. M. Davis & Sons, Inc. is now located outside of Wilmington and has opened offices in New Jersey and Maryland. The M. Davis vehicle fleet has grown from one Ford Model T pick-up truck to over 100 company owned vehicles. M. Davis & Sons, Inc. now offers a variety of services spanning the full range of industrial and commercial building services. Our workforce is comprised of highly skilled, licensed crane operators, welders, riggers, pipefitters, millwrights and machinists

who are equipped to handle any mechanical construction and maintenance project quickly, economically and safely. The M. Davis fabrication shop is a complete turnkey operation offering specialty sheet metal fabrication, repairs to ASME Code Section I boilers/pipe or Section VIII vessels/tanks, columns and reactors. M. Davis utilizes the latest in computer technology to design and specify various types of equipment and processing systems. Licensed in Delaware, Maryland, Pennsylvania and New Jersey, M. Davis and Sons' electrical trade professionals provide both experience and expertise. The M. Davis electrical group can handle electrical renovations, plant maintenance, branch circuits, troubleshooting, data wiring, high voltage load breaks, heat tracing and 35 KV installations. M. Davis & Sons' reputation for quality and safety is well known throughout the Delaware Valley. Our practices are governed by the PSM Safety Program and the Continuous Improvement principles of Total Quality Management. Today, M. Davis & Sons, Inc. continues to thrive and quality remains the cornerstone of the business. The M. Davis & Sons Team has always believed that no job is worth doing unless it is done exceptionally well. The diversity of our skills, combined with a solid commitment to workmanship, assures fully integrated industrial construction and maintenance services of the highest quality. From computer-aided design to general building maintenance, we promise fast turnaround, maximum production efficiency and strict adherence to safety and budgets. This level of performance has been the standard at M. Davis since our founding in 1870. Based at 200 Hadco Road, Wilmington, Delaware, M. Davis & Sons, Inc. is on call 24 hours a day, seven days a week.

W. L. Gore & Associates, Inc.

While consumers recognize the Gore name for the company's products – GORE-TEX® fabric and GLIDE® floss, among them — the Delaware community has known Gore for over forty years as a neighbor, innovator, and employer.

On its surface, the beginnings of W. L. Gore & Associates, Inc., in 1958 were not particularly unusual. It began like many family businesses: founders Bill and Vieve Gore started small, operating out of the basement of their Newark home. To test their product ideas, they pieced together whatever resources they found at hand. Their focus was what set them apart: they chose to pursue applications for fluoropolymers, versatile materials that they believed held great unexplored potential.

Their son, Bob, who was then a chemical engineering student at the University of Delaware, suggested the idea for an electronic cable insulated with the fluoropolymer polytetrafluoroethylene (PTFE). His suggestion became the company's first product and resulted in its first patent.

The company's first decade was marked by steady expansion. In 1961, the company moved out of the Gores' basement and into the first manufacturing plant, located on Paper Mill Road in Newark. By 1967, manufacturing had expanded to Germany, Scotland, and Flagstaff, Arizona.

A joint venture to manufacture products with a Japanese company followed in 1969. That same year a Gore product found its way to the moon: the Apollo 11 astronauts used a temperature-resistant Gore cable to conduct seismographic experiments on the moon's surface.

The year 1969 also saw a breakthrough which dramatically expanded the company's offerings and opened a wealth of new opportunities. Bob Gore discovered that rapidly stretching PTFE resulted in a remarkable material that offered many desirable new properties. Extremely strong, porous, waterproof, breathable, and possessed of excellent dielectric properties, Bob's discovery was named GORE-TEX® expanded PTFE.

In the early and mid-1970s, resulting new businesses sprang up in widely diverse markets. From sealant products for industrial pipes to implantable medical products for restoration of blood flow in the human body, Gore associates found uses for the new GORE-TEX® membrane and fibers in myriad applications.

GORE-TEX® fabric, the first waterproof yet breathable outerwear on the market, was born in that same period. It remains the most durably waterproof, very breathable and windproof fabric on the market, enabling wearers at work and play to stay dry in even the worst weather conditions.

The Gore name is now found on thousands of high performance products. They range from filtration products for virtually any environmental challenge to patches that repair heart defects and hernias. Gore chip modules and venting materials are found in the most sensitive components of computers, and the company's fibers are used in the outer layer of astronauts' space suits. No matter what the application, Gore products continue to be known today for their quality and technical benefits. The company is committed to invention and the challenge of bringing ever-better products to its customers.

That commitment is supported by another unique Gore creation: a work environment that lacks the barriers that sometimes impede more traditionally organized companies in their pursuit of innovation. Gore's corporate culture lacks titles and hierarchy. It is built upon direct, person-to-person communication rather than chains of command.

Because the culture gives Gore "associates" (not employees) the freedom to explore new ideas, it contributes directly to the generation of the company's product successes. It's also the reason the company has been repeatedly named one of the "100 Best Companies to Work For in America."

Today Gore is a worldwide presence, posting sales of well over $1 billion annually and employing thousands of associates in its 50 facilities around the world. While the company outgrew the basement workshop long ago, the same commitment to technical innovation that inspired Bill and Vieve Gore remains a constant among associates today.

The White Clay Creek valley outside Newark has been Gore's home since its founding. At right, a view of the creek where it runs along the company's recreation and nature area. ▶

Beebe Medical Center

Beebe Medical Center sits tucked along Savannah Road, across the street from a weathered, clapboard house that was its birthplace, a landmark that remains a constant reminder of a commitment made 82 years ago by two unassuming, physician brothers to the people of Lewes.

Drs. James and Richard Beebe were native sons of this, the first town in the first state. They loved Lewes, its people, and the amenities of living where the mouth of the Delaware Bay meets the Atlantic Ocean. They also knew their community lacked one very important asset: quality medical care, heretofore only available in the large cities to the north and south.

Both brothers graduated from Jefferson Medical College in Philadelphia, first James in 1906, then Richard in 1916. Bright and tenacious surgeons, job offers in big city practices were thrown at their feet.

For lesser men, the lure of practicing in the cradle of liberty would have proven to be an overpowering elixir. For the Drs. Beebe, coming home to Lewes was the only thing that mattered.

Both returned, manning a two-doctor practice that often meant house calls day and night, and placing the more serious patients onto a passing freight train enroute to Philadelphia and the surgical facilities of their alma mater.

A wealthy Wilmington couple, Benjamin F. and Helen M. Shaw, befriended the young doctors during one of their many vacations at Rehoboth Beach. Unsolicited, they donated $125,000 to build a permanent hospital which opened, at the Shaws' insistence, as the Beebe Hospital in 1921.

This was the first of what would be five phases of expansion over the next eight decades, including a second wing in 1927 built with donations from the Shaws. The Shaws were one of many philanthropic families who shared the Beebes' commitment to their community, a spirit that lives on in this rapidly growing area of Delaware. These monies were often matched–all, or in part– by state and federal healthcare dollars that were finding their way into Lewes.

In 1938, the Mary Thompson Wing was added; in 1962 construction began on the $1.5 million, five-story Lynch Wing, named for Harry W. Lynch, Sr., which opened in 1970; and in 1985, the five story Rollins Wing, named for entrepreneur John W. Rollins, opened.

Over the years, Beebe Medical Center changed a lot in its appearance, but not one iota in its philosophy of what quality healthcare should be.

Today, 75,000 year-round residents, and the hundreds of thousands of people who make the pilgrimage to the Lewes area each summer, look to Beebe for cost-effective, state-of-the-art healthcare.

Drawing on the resources of larger, nearby medical centers as referral points for major trauma cases and capital-intensive specialties like neonatology, and cardiac and neurosurgery, Beebe has responded to these demands, directing its focus to preventive and community-based medicine.

The hospital, whose patient satisfaction ranks in the top 20 percent of all hospitals nationwide, now boasts Sussex County's first radiation treatment program in the Tunnell Cancer Center; the Baylis Rehabilitation Center; the Hastings HeartCare Center; a summer-only emergency service in Millville; Mediquik, to care for beach-related maladies; and an 89-bed Lewes Convalescent Center Nursing Home. The 180-member physician staff serving the 138-bed hospital represents nearly every medical and surgical specialty and subspecialty.

Responding to needs in the outlying communities, Beebe has opened six growing community health centers, three outpatient testing centers, a pediatric practice in Lewes, and an adult daycare center.

In its infancy is Beebe's new managed-care plan, the Sussex Health Alliance. Construction also is expected to begin soon on a state-of-the-art outpatient and day treatment health campus just west of Lewes.

It is through the dedication of a board of directors committed to the beliefs

of Drs. James and Richard Beebe and the continuum of community leadership that Beebe Medical Center has remained focused for its journey into the next millennium.

Bancroft Construction Company

At the end of 1975, its first year in operation, Bancroft Construction Company posted revenues totalling $350,000. Today, Bancroft provides over $65,000,000 worth of Construction Management services per year and is one of Delaware's leading construction firms. *"Success"* to founder and CEO Stephen M. Mockbee means achieving the confidence of your customers, the trust of your employees, and the respect of your community. Every aspect of Bancroft's strategic planning process leads back to one of these core values in some way.

For example, Bancroft's Safety Program was designed to eliminate risk for Owners through a comprehensive system of processes and procedures that is monitored on-site by Bancroft's in-house Safety Management Team. The program is recognized consistently by local and national organizations dedicated to safe practices in the workplace. Bancroft personnel have also consulted with companies such as Proctor and Gamble and the U.S. Army Corps of Engineers in their efforts to improve safety policies. This is just one of the many programs that Bancroft has developed and implemented to serve the best interests of its customers, employees, and community.

One of Bancroft's first contracts was to renovate space for sculptor Charles Parks at 44 Bancroft Mills, a historic mill building on the Brandywine River. Shortly after completing the Parks' renovation, Bancroft rented space in the same building. Eventually, Bancroft purchased 5300 square feet adjacent to Mr. Parks' studio. In addition to the mill location, Bancroft maintains satellite offices to manage on-site program administration as warranted. And in June 1998, Bancroft opened a second corporate office near Greenhill Avenue to support its ever expanding commercial, institutional, and industrial operations.

Bancroft's workload reflects its diverse client base and showcases its expertise. From the $57,000,000 laboratory, office, and research facility for one of Delaware's high profile corporations to the Harley Davidson retail, museum, and restaurant complex for an enterprising entrepreneur, Bancroft specializes in customizing its approach to the needs and challenges of each project.

A recent award winning project called for the conversion of a 1937 estate home into a corporate center with exceptionally high technological capabilities. A landmark ordinance, established by the Historic Review Board and County Council, mandated that both the interior and exterior historical integrity of the residence and its grounds be retained despite a tight budget. The success of the project demonstrated how adaptive reuse of massive estates is a desirable way to preserve land and buildings that might otherwise succumb to subdivision and redevelopment.

Other projects such as neighborhood centers and educational facilities mean opportunity for the larger community. They help generate benefactors for similar projects when the building's contribution to the overall quality of life is recognized. The construction of the Walnut Street YMCA on its original 60 year old site represents an especially ambitious venture. It is the first urban YMCA to be rehabilitated in the United States in over ten years. Fundraising, existing conditions, an efficient design that would adequately accommodate future generations, orchestrating 40,000 square feet of construction in a confined, partially residential area - all presented considerations that could easily derail the project. But funding commitments from corporations to school children and creative solutions for the many logistical criteria helped keep the project moving forward as the neighborhood and the nation watched closely. For Bancroft, it is not about just constructing a building, it is an example of what is possible when the talents and the vision of caring people converge.

Bancroft Construction Company has undergone a tremendous metamorphosis in the past 28 years. The advanced scheduling, project coordination, and estimating technology have replaced cumbersome and time intensive management methods with a sophisticated science. In addition to Bancroft's fully equipped in-house learning center and a Management Information Systems department, Bancroft personnel regularly attend seminars and workshops to stay current with the latest technological capabilities. The technology revolution cannot be underrated; it affords our customers exceptional control over costs, time, and quality levels, reliable forecasting, and immediate response to issues that develop throughout the life cycle of a project.

Forecasts indicate a surge for the construction industry as dedicated funds and commitments for new buildings and expansions are declared. But as important as Bancroft's systems and strategies are, they are not the key to Bancroft's future. It is the people behind the systems and strategies – evaluating, anticipating, implementing, with enthuisasm and commitment – who will continue Bancroft's reputation for superior and consistent service. Because the people of Bancroft are its most valuable asset, Bancroft is dedicated to promoting opportunities at all levels within the construction industry. Bancroft offers a variety of mentoring programs that expose young people to the many career choices available. Bancroft, in conjunction with the Delaware Vo-Tech School System, sponsors a Co-Op Program for those interested in administrative or accounting functions. Full time employment for qualified candidates is an option after twelve months. There is also a Job Shadowing Program, a Work Site Learning Program, a summer intern program for college students, and a Career Awareness Program (with Salesianum High School) for students particularly interested in Construction Management positions. Mentoring enables Bancroft to train, teach, stay open to innovation, and ultimately contributes to the stability and excellence of Bancroft's customer service program.

The Brandywine River as seen from Bancroft Construction Company's corporate headquarters. ▶

Standard Chlorine of Delaware, Inc.

Standard Chlorine of Delaware, Inc. has been an integral part of Delaware for over 30 years. Situated along Governor Lea Road in Delaware City Industrial Complex, SCD employs more than 130 specially trained, highly skilled men and women who take pride in their jobs and community. With over 1400 years of combined service, these employees are the backbone of SCD's continued success and future growth.

NEW BEGINNINGS

In 1998, Charter Oak Partners, a private investment partnership, acquired Standard Chlorine of Delaware. Its new management is committed to improving and enhancing Site operations to meet and exceed all applicable local, state and federal rules and regulations. A leading manufacturer of halogenated compounds, SCD is renewing its commitment to on-time, quality products, with a strong focus on customer satisfaction and competitive pricing.

PRODUCT PORTFOLIO

A world leader in the markets it serves, SCD manufactures a broad range of organic intermediates used to manufacture myriad consumer products, including pharmaceuticals, plastics and agrochemicals as well as various industrial applications such as water treatment, cement cleaning, steel pickling, food processing, dyes and heat transfer materials.

VISION FOR THE FUTURE

A newer, more progressive entity, SCD is positioned to move into the 21st century with a new vision, new products and a renewed commitment to be the quality leader in the markets it serves. SCD will continue to improve manufacturing operations by implementing stringent process control procedures and by refining processes to meet the constantly changing market demands.

SCD is investing millions of dollars to improve processes that recycle and reuse byproduct compounds, thus reducing or eliminating waste and emissions from the Site. The Site is constructing modern raw material unloading facilities and installing state-of-the-art high-efficiency distillation equipment. SCD is committed to being a leading Corporate citizen in the State of Delaware and a role model in safe manufacturing practices.

SCD ensures that its employees are continually trained in the latest technology and safe manufacturing processes and procedures available. SCD is one of eight Delaware companies involved in developing the Process Operators' degree program offered at Delaware Technical and Community College. In addition, all process control operators and relief operators participated in a workshop designed to ensure they possess the level of skills necessary to do their jobs safely, effectively and efficiently. The workshop integrates safety and environmental concerns as well as workplace safety and environmental responsibility, incorporating the chemical industry's Responsible Care® program and OSHA's Process Safety Management regulations. Safety, Quality and Skills training for employees is an integral part of doing business in a global marketplace.

Every successful company needs dedicated, loyal employees, and SCD is no exception. A majority of the Company's employees have spent their entire careers with SCD. The Company's outstanding long-term service record is due to its "open door" policy. Beginning with upper management, employees are encouraged to provide feedback on ways to improve performance. Employees play a critical role in the Company's continued success, working as a team to ensure safe working conditions for their colleagues and visitors and a safe environment for Site neighbors.

SCD prides itself on constantly looking for ways to improve its operations as well as its community involvement. The Company is an active member of Delaware City's CAER (Community Awareness and Emergency Response) initiative. In addition, SCD orchestrates tours and presentations for local schools as well as funding for the annual Delaware Chemical Industry Council Science Olympiad. To complement the Company's philosophy of "giving something back to the community" in which it operates, SCD's employees are involved in numerous community activities and services, from volunteer firefighters and paramedics to community clean-up days and Meals On Wheels for senior citizens.

Dynamic, prosperous, determined and bright . . .words that describe SCD's future--a future filled with steady growth, dedicated employees, new product development, improved customer satisfaction, competitive pricing and unparalleled pride in being a leading quality supplier of organic intermediates to meet the needs of the 21st century and beyond.

SCD's employees are the backbone of the Company's continued success. ▶

Snyder, Crompton & Associates

Snyder, Crompton & Associates was founded in 1954 and is currently one of the more reputable construction companies in the Brandywine Valley. SC&A performs Construction Management Services and General Contracting for many of the Fortune 500 companies and is still privately held. The three shareholders of SC&A take a personal approach still to this day by being personally involved in every project to varying degrees, therefore maintaining customer satisfaction. A primary focus within the company is to create a team approach when working with a client by involving the customer, SC&A staff, architectural and engineering firms when beginning the process of constructability.

The company has, over the years, worked in Delaware, Southeast Pennsylvania, Northern Maryland and South Jersey for many varied clients. The types of work have ranged from custom residential, medical, R&D, pharmaceuticals, as well as clean rooms, x-ray and bio-hazardous/infectious facilities. With this type of work and customer base, the organization has performed upwards of 90% of its volume on a negotiated basis which is a large tribute for return business and customer satisfaction.

Although SC&A has remained relatively small ($45 million sales with 75 employees), it has become a large name to its customers because of the "hands-on" approach and commitment to quality and value. Over the past fifteen years, the customer base has primarily been commercial in nature with a steady, controlled growth. SC&A has also on staff personnel working full time in support of: Safety Compliance, Mechanical and Electrical Quality Assurance/ Quality Control, and Commissioning personnel.

The Delaware Center for Horticulture project exemplifies our commitment to quality and value.

With the Brandywine Park as a back-drop, Snyder, Crompton & Associates, Inc. renovated and utilized an existing Parks and Recreation maintenance building complex. New uses include multi-purpose spaces, job training facilities, administrative offices, horticultural library, retail space, and demonstration gardens.

The old brick building structure was preserved. Trusses, heavy timber, and window treatment were painted to enliven the space. Each program area is mechanically zoned separately so areas of the building can be tempered when not in use. The mechanical zones can be completely turned off and windows opened when temperatures are favorable.

This renovation provides an attractive functional and energy efficient headquarters to serve Delaware residents.

Andersen Consulting LLP

Andersen Consulting was not founded in Delaware, but, since 1996 has established a "home base" for its global chemicals industry segment in the state. At that time, Andersen Consulting joined with DuPont, one of the most highly respected chemical companies in the world, to create the DuPont IT Alliance, a 10-year relationship designed to implement far-reaching change for DuPont and the chemical industry. The firm pursues this goal by providing to its clients services and solutions designed to advance their business objectives.

Andersen Consulting and DuPont are a natural pair; both have been built on principles of change and innovation. DuPont's vision of reinvention, discovery, and change began in 1802, when the company was founded near Wilmington. Andersen Consulting's mission, "helping its clients change to be more successful," has guided its activities since it was established as a distinct business in 1989. Though almost 200 years span those dates, the concept of change as a business solution fits the two organizations, and indeed, has propelled both to enduring success.

Andersen Consulting has a history of teaming with clients like DuPont who have the courage and vision to seek out change and make it happen. Whether helping an organization to change its shape after a merger or guiding an expansion into global markets, the firm's aim is not merely to help clients cope with change, but to go further, and make far-reaching change an integral part of an organization's new strategy for success. Such change permeates an organization to its very core. Andersen Consulting helps leading organizations realize the full potential of technology to create new business capabilities, pursue new strategies and dramatically improve performance.

At the same time, Andersen Consulting has demonstrated that it, too, has the courage to change — uprooting its own established structures and hierarchies to create a new global organization that can speedily deliver knowledge and the new and innovative approaches to its clients anywhere in the world.

With its newest facility in Delaware, Andersen Consulting has taken the concept of far-reaching change to the architectural realm. Built as a model for the consulting firm of the future, the facility houses professionals who bring both the industry insights and global, integrated capabilities which help enable chemical companies to compete successfully. It does so within a structure designed like a small city, with an open work environment that fosters cooperation and creativity. Officially opened on March 9, 1998, Andersen Consulting's Chemical Industry Center of Excellence has transformed a Wilmington landmark — the Wanamaker's Department Store — into an architectural achievement where innovation can flourish.

The center showcases Andersen Consulting's ability to provide DuPont with services which enhance shareholder value, and perhaps most importantly, the Center has been designed to inspire creative energy, and to help its professionals "think outside the box," when designing and delivering services for DuPont and the chemical industry at large. "Chemical companies around the world can now look to Wilmington for industry-specific business solutions," said Delaware Governor Thomas R. Carper, who attended the opening of the center with senior officials of Andersen Consulting. "We are proud to welcome Andersen Consulting's state-of-the-art chemical industry center of excellence to Delaware. This addition to our economic base will make us an even more attractive place to do business."

Since locating in Wilmington, Andersen Consulting also has been committed to playing a leading role in the Delaware community. The firm worked with many Wilmington businesses throughout various stages of its facility's development and transformation. And numerous senior executives are participating on state task forces. Over time, the firm's services are certain to foster additional employment opportunities. All of which supports Andersen Consulting's commitment to becoming part of the fabric of the Delaware community.

Delaware Scenes

◀◀◀ **Autumn at Brandywine Creek State Park**
◀◀ **Winter at Rockford Park**
◀ **Spring blossoms at Rockwood Museum**
Sunset at Bombay Hook ▶